GIVING
IN
AMERICA

GIVING IN AMERICA

Toward a Stronger Voluntary Sector

Report of the Commission on Private
Philanthropy and Public Needs

TABLE OF CONTENTS

  *1. That to increase inducements for charitable giving, all taxpay-
  ers who take the standard deduction should also be permitted
  to deduct charitable contributions as an additional, itemized
  deduction.*

2. *That an additional inducement to charitable giving should be provided to low- and middle-income taxpayers. Toward this end, the Commission proposes that a "double deduction" be instituted for families with incomes of less than $15,000 a year; they would be allowed to deduct twice what they give in computing their income taxes. For those families with incomes between $15,000 and $30,000, the Commission proposes a deduction of 150 per cent of their giving.*

That income deducted for charitable giving should be excluded from any minimum tax provision.

That the appreciated property allowance within the charitable deduction be basically retained but amended to eliminate any possibility of personal financial gain through tax-deductible charitable giving.

That the charitable bequest deduction be retained in its present form.

That corporations set as a minimum goal, to be reached no later than 1980, the giving to charitable purposes of 2 per cent of pre-tax net income. Moreover, the Commission believes that the national commission proposed in this report should consider as a priority concern additional measures to stimulate corporate giving.

2. *That to discourage unnecessary accumulation of income, a flat payout rate of 5 per cent of principal be fixed by Congress for private foundations and a lower rate for other endowed tax-exempt organizations.*

3. *That a system of federal regulation be established for interstate charitable solicitations and that intrastate solicitations be more effectively regulated by state governments.*

4. *That as a federal enforcement tool against abuses by tax-exempt organizations, and to protect these organizations themselves, sanctions appropriate to the abuses should be enacted as well as forms of administrative or judicial review of the principal existing sanction—revocation of an organization's exempt status.*

That nonprofit organizations, other than foundations, be allowed the same freedoms to attempt to influence legislation as are business corporations and trade associations, that toward this end Congress remove the current limitation on such activity by charitable groups eligible to receive tax-deductible gifts.

That a permanent national commission on the nonprofit sector be established by Congress.

PREFACE

The Commission on Private Philanthropy and Public Needs was established in November, 1973, as a privately initiated, privately funded citizens' panel with two broad objectives:

To study the role of both philanthropic giving in the United States and that area through which giving is principally channeled, the voluntary, "third" sector of American society.

To make recommendations to the voluntary sector, to Congress and to the American public at large concerning ways in which the sector and the practice of private giving can be strengthened and made more effective.

The Commission's objectives reflect a conviction that giving and voluntary, public-oriented activity—the components of "philanthropy" as broadly defined—play a central role in American life but that the continuation of this role cannot be taken for granted. For the sector's economic durability has been brought into question by the mounting financial difficulties of many voluntary organizations and nonprofit institutions. At the same time, two of the main institutional underpinnings of philanthropic giving—private foundations and charitable tax deductions—have been politically challenged. Congressional hearings leading up to the Tax Reform Act of 1969 as well as the act itself showed that these underpinnings had become fair targets of criticism and of legislative change.

The Commission came into existence in large measure because of the initiative of John D. Rockefeller 3rd and the encouragement of several governmental figures, including the chairman then of the House Ways and Means Committee, Wilbur D. Mills, Secretary of the Treasury George P. Shultz and Under Secretary William E. Simon, who was subsequently Shultz's successor. The Commission's membership was drawn

1

from a broad spectrum of American society and has included religious and labor leaders, former cabinet officers, representatives of minority groups, executives of foundations and corporations—men and women with wide ranging and differing viewpoints.

It became apparent even before the Commission was formally established that it would need and would have to develop for itself a great deal of one particularly scarce commodity in the areas it was looking at—information. A meeting of tax experts, economists and sociologists assembled to discuss the research needs of the proposed commission in August, 1973, and reached a quick consensus: that there was a paucity of existing data and analysis on giving patterns, about tax effects on giving, about the relative roles of government and nonprofit organizations, about many basic questions surrounding giving and nonprofit activity. A major research task was clearly cut out for any group looking into this area.

Gabriel G. Rudney was granted leave of absence as assistant director of the Treasury Department's Office of Tax Analysis to serve as research director of the Commission. Jeanne Moore has worked since the Commission's early days as the Commission's executive assistant and coordinator of its vast flow of documents and correspondence. Advising the Commission and aiding in the direction of its research has been an Advisory Committee made up of more than 100 experts in the fields of economics, law, sociology and taxation, plus representatives of many philanthropic and nonprofit areas, from higher education to environmental activism. More fully involved in the Commission's work have been the Commission's consultants, some in general and some in special capacities, many of whom have regularly taken part in the Commission's deliberations. However, the Commission's report, it should be noted, is the Commission's own and does not necessarily reflect the views of any consultants or advisors.

The Commission has sponsored in the course of its two years in operation no fewer than 85 studies on various aspects of philanthropy and nonprofit activity, including individual reports on all the major areas of charitable nonprofit activity; extensive analysis of the laws and precedents, in the United

States and abroad, that govern the practice of philanthropy and "third sector" activity; and reports on philanthropy in five cities in different regions of the country.

A sample survey was commissioned to probe taxpayers' giving practices and attitudes. The largest such survey ever conducted, it involved lengthy interviews with close to 3,000 individuals, representing a cross-section of American contributors, and non-contributors. The survey was run by the Survey Research Center of the University of Michigan. The U.S. Treasury Department aided in the preparation of the survey and the U.S. Census Bureau conducted one third of the actual interviews.

Computerized econometric analysis of tax and income data was made for the Commission in an effort to determine what, if any, effect the charitable deduction had on the amount of giving people did. From the relationships found in this analysis, simulations were constructed to project the possible effect of modifications and expansions of the deduction and the effect of alternative proposals for stimulating giving.

Meetings and discussions were held in different parts of the country involving concerned citizens and leaders in every field related to the Commission's areas of study; gatherings of experts in various technical subjects helped frame the technical issues considered by the Commission and also planned and reviewed research. Government agencies, particularly the Department of Health, Education and Welfare and the Internal Revenue Service, were consulted extensively in areas of their expertise and concern.

In planning both its written research and the discussions it sponsored, the Commission has made a conscious effort to practice the openness that, in its report, it preaches for all nonprofit organizations, openness inward to a wide variety of viewpoints and openness outward to observation of its own, hardly monolithic deliberations. For example, partly in answer to criticism that the Commission's membership represented donor interests more than donee interests within the world of philanthropy, the Commission supported the establishment of a "donee group," which was linked to the Commission and which sponsored a number of studies and critiques for—and of—the Commission. This group has had, we believe, a valuable influence on the Commission's thinking and on its report.

The Commission has itself assembled in many lengthy sessions, and individual Commission members have taken part in other Commission-sponsored meetings as well. Many of the issues that the Commission has deliberated on and attempted to find a consensus on have not been easy ones. A broad and unequivocal consensus exists within the Commission, as it clearly does within American society at large, as to the desirability of voluntary giving and voluntary organizations. However, profound and often sensitive social, economic and political concerns lie barely beneath the surface of any consideration of philanthropy and nonprofit activity in the mid-1970's, among them concerns about the power of personal and corporate wealth, about the role of government, about the quality of equality and the definition of equity. Such concerns, coming at a time of national self-questioning, after a decade of social ferment, offer no simple solutions or resolutions.

So, inevitably perhaps, the Commission's recommendations for dealing with perceived imperfections, inequities or simple insufficiencies in the areas it has examined have not always been unanimous, not without dissent. Yet the Commission is confident that in its own quest and in attempting to resolve its own uncertainties, it has furthered considerably the knowledge of a dimly known region of American life. The Commission hopes further that it has set in motion a process of further examination of this region, which, the Commission believes, has too long been taken for granted and must now be attended to, and perhaps vigorously reinforced, if it is to continue to play the major role in American life that it has throughout the nation's history.

It is with this confidence, and this hope, that this Commission offers for consideration this report on its findings and its recommendations. Soon to be published separately is a compendium of all reports and studies undertaken for the Commission.

We are deeply grateful to more than 700 organizations and individuals for their generous and indispensable support of the Commission, which has depended on private giving to finance its meetings, researches and publications. Special thanks are due in turn to Commission member Philip M. Klutznick, and to John J. Schwartz and his colleagues in the American Association of Fund-Raising Counsel for their diligent fund-raising efforts.

John H. Filer, Chairman
Leonard L. Silverstein, Executive Director

INTRODUCTION
and
SUMMARY

INTRODUCTION AND
SUMMARY

Few aspects of American society are more characteristically, more famously American than the nation's array of voluntary organizations, and the support in both time and money that is given to them by its citizens. Our country has been decisively different in this regard, historian Daniel Boorstin observes, "from the beginning." As the country was settled, "communities existed before governments were there to care for public needs." The result, Boorstin says, was that "voluntary collaborative activities" were set up to provide basic social services. Government followed later.

The practice of attending to community needs outside of government has profoundly shaped American society and its institutional framework. While in most other countries, major social institutions such as universities, hospitals, schools, libraries, museums and social welfare agencies are state-run and state-funded, in the United States many of the same organizations are privately controlled and voluntarily supported. The institutional landscape of America is, in fact, teeming with nongovernmental, noncommercial organizations, all the way from some of the world's leading educational and cultural institutions to local garden clubs, from politically powerful national associations to block associations—literally millions of groups in all. This vast and varied array is, and has long been widely recognized as, part of the very fabric of American life. It reflects a national belief in the philosophy of pluralism and in the profound importance to society of individual initiative.

Underpinning the virtual omnipresence of voluntary organizations, and a form of individual initiative in its own right, is the practice—in the case of many Americans, the deeply ingrained habit—of philanthropy, of private giving, which provides the resource base for voluntary organizations. Between money gifts and the contributions of time and labor in the

9

form of volunteer work, giving is valued at more than $50 billion a year, according to Commission estimates.

These two interrelated elements, then, are sizable forces in American society, far larger than in any other country. And they have contributed immeasurably to this country's social and scientific progress. On the ledger of recent contributions are such diverse advances as the creation of noncommercial "public" television, the development of environmental, consumerist and demographic consciousness, community-oriented museum programs, the protecting of land and landmarks from the often heedless rush of "progress." The list is endless and still growing; both the number and deeds of voluntary organizations are increasing. "Americans are forever forming associations," wrote de Tocqueville. They still are: tens of thousands of environmental organizations have sprung up in the last few years alone. Private giving is growing, too, at least in current dollar amounts.

Changes and Challenges

Yet, while the value of philanthropy and voluntary organizations, their past and present achievements, is hardly questioned by Americans, and while by international comparisons these two expressions of the voluntary spirit are of unmatched dimensions, a major overall conclusion of this Commission must be that there are profound, and in some areas troubling, shifts happening in the interrelated realms of voluntary organization and philanthropy, changes that reflect, as these quintessential elements in American society must, broader churnings in the society as a whole. These changes present both practical and philosophical challenges to established patterns of voluntary activity and philanthropy.

The practical challenges are suggested by the stark fact that while many new organizations are being born in the voluntary sector, since 1969 nearly 150 private colleges—representing one of the oldest and largest areas of voluntary activity throughout American history—have closed down. Among the philosophical challenges are those facing the main governmental encouragement of private giving—the charitable deduction in the federal income tax—which is being questioned on grounds of equity.

10

FINDINGS

The Commission's findings—about both the enduring virtues of nonprofit activity and philanthropic giving and about current challenges to established patterns within these areas—can be summarized in four broad observations:

1. *The voluntary sector is a large and vital part of American society, more important today than ever. But the sector is undergoing economic strains that predate and are generally more severe than the troubles of the economy as a whole.*

According to recent extrapolations, there may be as many as six million organizations in American's voluntary sector (also referred to in this report as the third sector—third after government and business—and as the private nonprofit sector, or simply nonprofit sector for short). One out of every ten service workers in the United States is employed by a nonprofit organization, one out of every six professional workers. One ninth of all property is owned by voluntary organizations.

The last estimate encompasses groups such as labor unions and chambers of commerce, which serve primarily the economic interests of their members. The somewhat smaller part of the voluntary sector that has been the focus of the Commission's attention is defined for most Commission purposes by Section 501(c)(3) of the Internal Revenue Code, which covers organizations that are both tax exempt and eligible to receive tax-deductible gifts. The code specifically designates charitable, religious, scientific, literary and educational organizations.

The Commission estimates that revenues in these areas, including both government and private funds, add up to around $80 billion a year. This amount does not include non-money resources, such as volunteer work and free corporate services. When these are added in, it is estimated that the voluntary sector accounts for over $100 billion in money and other resources annually.

These are impressive figures, but the significance of the third sector in today's society is found ultimately in less quantifiable dimensions.

Recent tremors in the nation's governance have strengthened the deeply rooted American conviction that no single institutional structure should exercise a monopoly on filling public needs, that reliance on government alone to fill such needs not only saps the spirit of individual initiative but risks making human values subservient to institutional ones, individual and community purposes subordinate to bureaucratic conveniences or authoritarian dictates. Thus, the third sector's role as an addition to government and, in many areas, an alternative and even counterbalance to government, has possibly never been more important; the basic rationale of the third sector in the philosophy of pluralism has possibly never been more pertinent. Also, in a society increasingly dominated by giant and impersonal institutions of business and government, voluntary organizations, generally less giant and more personal, provide arenas within which the individual can exercise personal initiative and influence on the course of events around him or her.

Economic Strains

The vital role of the voluntary sector in today's society must be viewed, however, against a background of mounting financial and economic strains that threaten the sector's ability to adequately perform this role.

The recent economy-wide pressures of inflation and recession have intensified strains that have been felt by the voluntary sector for a number of years. Even in the late 1960's, when the economy was booming, one major survey of the philanthropic landscape found matters bad and getting worse. "Without important new sources of funds amounting to many billions of dollars," the report concluded, "our society will feel the full force of what can be called the charitable crisis of the 1970's."

Acute crisis describes the state of many parts of the nonprofit sector today. The existence of whole areas within the sector may be threatened.

One Commission study asserts that it is not "idle speculation to talk of the disappearance of the liberal arts college." Another study says that "in the long run, if the economic trends continue, the vast majority of nonpublic schools seem doomed, the exceptions being schools enjoying the support of the well-to-do or heavy subsidies from a few remaining religious groups with conservative theologies or strong ethnic emphasis." Social service organizations have been slashing their budgets and reducing their staffs in order to stay afloat. In a number of cases, they have gone out of business entirely. And nonprofit arts organizations, in many cases, are surviving only through large infusions of government funds.

The problems arise on both the income and expense sides of the ledger.

Extraordinary increases in costs, many of them beyond the control of nonprofit causes, are a major factor. Costs for many nonprofit organizations have been going up far more rapidly than in the economy as a whole for a number of years. Since 1960, medical care prices have risen half again as fast as consumer prices in general. Higher education costs rose about 76 per cent between 1963-64 and 1973-74, as compared with 49 per cent for the economy-wide cost-of-living index.

The prevailing financial pattern of the nonprofit sector has become one not only of uncommonly higher costs, but of more resources required for old problems and new solutions, and of more users needing greater aggregate subsidies for the non-profit services that they consume. In addition, new and less traditional groups, such as those oriented toward urban and racial problems, environmental and consumer organizations, and other politically and legally activist groups, have been adding their claim for pieces of the philanthropic pie. And the pie has not been growing in terms of the real purchasing power of private contributions.

2. *Giving in America involves an immense amount of time and money, is the fundamental underpinning of the voluntary sector, encompasses a wide diversity of relationships between donor, donations and donee, and is not keeping pace.*

Most giving—79 per cent in 1974—comes from living individuals, and the main focus of the Commission's research has been on such giving. The Commission's largest single research effort was a Commission-sponsored sample survey of 2,917 taxpayers

13

conducted jointly by the University of Michigan's Survey Research Center and by the U.S. Census Bureau. Extensive questioning of respondents was conducted in 1974, covering giving for the previous year. In 1973, according to projections based on the respondents' answers, individuals may have given as much as $26 billion.

In addition, nearly six billion womanhours and manhours of volunteer work were contributed to nonprofit organizations in 1973, the survey indicates, and the total value placed on this contributed labor is another $26 billion. (Bequests accounted for $2.07 billion in 1974, foundations for $2.11 billion and corporations for $1.25 billion in direct dollar giving.)

Estimating the sources of giving by individuals is still more art than science, but even by conservative reckonings, $50 billion a year is the very large round-number total of the value of contributed time and money in the mid-1970's. A disproportionate amount of giving comes from contributors with the highest income, at least 13 per cent of individual giving from this 1 per cent of the population. Yet at the same time the bulk of giving, more than half, comes from households with incomes below $20,000.

Other Commission findings: college graduates give six times as much on the average as do those with only high school educations. Small town residents give more than city dwellers. The married give more than the single, the old more than the young. The giving of time was also found to correlate closely with the giving of money; the contributor of one is likely to be a contributor of the other.

Where the Giving Goes

Where does the giving go? The largest single recipient area is religion. Studies by the Interfaith Research Committee of the Commission indicate that religious giving may be larger than generally estimated, and at the same time the committee found that a sizable share of religious giving—one out of five dollars— is ultimately given in turn by religious organizations to other, non-sacramental categories of recipient. The estimated breakdown of giving in terms of ultimate recipient, in 1973, was:

religion, $10.28 billion; education, $4.41 billion; health, $3.89 billion; social welfare, $2.07 billion; arts, humanities, civic and public causes, $1.67 billion; and all other, $3.19 billion.

When incomes of givers and kinds of recipients are looked at together, a pronounced pattern is evident. Lower-income contributors give even more predominantly to religion than do Americans as a whole; higher incomes give mainly to education, hospitals and cultural institutions.

Not Keeping Pace

While philanthropy plays a far larger role in the U.S. than in any other country, a disturbing finding is that the purchasing power of giving did not keep pace with the growth of the economy through the expansive years of the 1960's and early 1970's and that in recent years it has fallen off absolutely when discounted for inflation.

The American Association of Fund-Raising Counsel estimates that giving has dropped from 1.98 per cent of the gross national product in 1969 to 1.80 per cent in 1974. A Commission-sponsored study by economist Ralph Nelson concludes that, as a proportion of personal income, giving by individuals dropped by about 15 per cent between 1960 and 1972. The relative sluggishness of giving has been even more pronounced when looked at alongside the growth of government spending. In 1960, private giving amounted to one ninth of expenditures by all levels of government (not counting defense spending); in 1974, giving added up to less than one fourteenth of government spending. The Commission's studies indicate, significantly, that it is in the $10,000 to $25,000 range that giving has fallen off the most in recent years.

The dropoff in giving is by no means uniform. Giving to religion has declined most of all, falling from 49 to 43 per cent of all giving between 1964 and 1974, paralleling a drop in church attendance and in parochial school enrollments. Meantime, giving to civic and cultural causes has actually risen. And volunteer work has gone up markedly according to government surveys conducted in 1965 and in 1974. The success of some causes in regularly raising large sums suggests that the spirit of

15

giving may not be fading so much as shifting its focus, even if the level of giving, of money at least, clearly has declined, by virtually every barometer.

3. *Decreasing levels of private giving, increasing costs of non-profit activity and broadening expectations for health, education and welfare services as basic entitlements of citizenship have led to the government's becoming a principal provider of programs and revenues in many areas once dominated by private philanthropy. And government's growing role in these areas poses fundamental questions about the autonomy and basic functioning of private nonprofit organizations and institutions.*

As a direct supporter of nonprofit organizations and activities, government today contributes almost as much as all sources of private philanthropy combined. In 1974, Commission studies indicate, government contributed about $23 billion to nonprofit organizations, compared to $25 billion from private giving. In addition, government has absorbed many philanthropic functions or services, either through the spread of public institutions and agencies that are counterparts of private organizations or through social programs that render philanthropic services and functions obsolete or redundant.

The growing role of government in what have been considered philanthropic activities is evident at every turn in the nonprofit sector. In medical and health spending, for example, the federal government was spending only 15 per cent more than private philanthropy in 1930. In 1973, it was spending nearly seven times as much. In 1960 about two thirds of all institutions of higher learning were private; today the proportion is closer to one half. In 1950 more than one half of all higher-education students were enrolled in private institutions; today the ratio is around one quarter.

The most massive change has occurred in relation to the poor, the unemployed, the aged, the infirm—largely because of Social Security legislation enacted in the 1930's. The impact of this legislation can be seen in the fact that in 1974 more than $90 billion was dispensed in old-age, survivors, disability and health insurance, and various forms of welfare assistance. Pri-

16

vate philanthropy, by comparison, distributed around $2.3 billion in the whole "social welfare" category.

Along with this change has come an ever increasing involvement of government in the finances of nonprofit organizations themselves. The nonprofit sector has, in fact, become an increasingly mixed realm—part private, part public—in much the same sense that the profit-making sector has; and this trend poses a major dilemma. On the one hand, government money is needed and may even be a matter of life or death for many organizations as the amount of their private funding has advanced slowly or even declined. On the other hand, government money comes with strings attached, however invisible or unintentional they may be. The more an organization depends on government money for survival, the less "private" it is, and the less immune to political processes and priorities.

Various methods have evolved in recent years to "buffer" government funds from political purse-string influence. But, as many studies made for the Commission suggest, perhaps the most effective, and most possible, safeguard of autonomy is to have more than one purse to draw from. The presence of a firm core of private support, however small, in a private organization that gets major public funding can be of crucial importance in determining whether the managers of the organizations regard themselves, and behave, as independent operators or as civil servants.

In stressing the importance of private giving, however, the Commission recognizes that giving itself is influenced by government through the tax system and that some of the most debated issues concerning relations of government and the voluntary sector revolve around how the tax system is structured and how it affects donors and donees.

4. *Our society has long encouraged "charitable" nonprofit activity by excluding it from certain tax obligations. But the principal tax encouragement of giving to nonprofit organizations—the charitable deduction in personal income taxes—has been both challenged from some quarters in recent years on grounds of equity and eroded by expansion of the standard deduction.*

The charitable deduction has been part of the tax law since 1917, four years after the income tax itself became a basic fixture of American life. It was instituted to sustain the level of giving in the face of new steep tax rates and because it was held that personal income that went to charitable purposes should not be taxed because it did not enrich the giver. These remain the two principal rationales of the charitable deduction, under which a contributor can subtract the amount of yearly giving from income upon which income taxes are computed. In recent years, however, partly as a result of a growing tendency to look at tax immunities as forms of government subsidy, the charitable deduction has been criticized, along with other personal income tax deductions, as inequitable. This is because, under the progressive income tax, the higher the deductor's tax bracket, the greater the tax savings he or she receives from taking a deduction. Thus, high tax bracket contributors have a significantly greater incentive to give than those at the other end of the income scale.

At the same time that the charitable deduction is being challenged philosophically, it is being eroded, in very concrete terms, by liberalizations of the standard deduction, the income tax provision that allows taxpayers to deduct a set amount or a proportion of their income in lieu of taking specific, itemized deductions. The maximum standard deduction has increased greatly in recent years—from $1,000 for a couple in 1970 to $2,600 in 1975. This has so diminished the advantage of taking itemized deductions that as of 1975's returns less than one third of all taxpayers are expected to be taking the charitable deduction.

RECOMMENDATIONS

Such are the main dimensions, trends and issues that the Commission's extensive research has uncovered or illuminated. These findings provide the background for the Commission's recommendations, among the major ones of which are those below. They fall into three categories: proposals involving taxes and giving; those that affect the "philanthropic process," the

18

interaction between donors, donees and the public; and a proposal for a permanent commission on the nonprofit sector.

I. TAXES AND GIVING

The Commission examined the existing governmental inducement to giving and considered several proposed alternatives, including tax credits for giving and matching grant systems. In doing so, it kept these six objectives in mind:

—To increase the number of people who contribute significantly to and participate in nonprofit activities.

—To increase the amount of giving.

—To increase the inducements to giving by those in low- and middle-income brackets.

—To preserve private choice in giving.

—To minimize income losses of nonprofit organizations that depend on the current pattern of giving.

—To be as "efficient" as possible. In other words, any stimulus to giving should not cost significantly more in foregone government revenue than the amount of giving actually stimulated.

A. Continuing the Deduction

In light of these criteria, the Commission believes that the charitable deduction should be retained and added onto rather than replaced by another form of governmental encouragement to giving. The Commission affirms the basic philosophical rationale of the deduction, that giving should not be taxed because, unlike other uses of income, it does not enrich the disburser. Also, the deduction is a proven mechanism familiar to donor and donee, easy to administrate and less likely than credits or matching grants to run afoul of constitutional prohibitions as far as donations to religious organizations are concerned.

The deduction has been shown, furthermore, to be a highly "efficient" inducement. Computerized econometric analyses based on available tax and income data were made for the Commission and they indicate that for every dollar of taxes uncollected because of the charitable deduction, more than one dollar in giving is stimulated. The Commission's sample survey of taxpayers also indicates that itemizers who take the charitable deduction give substantially more, at every income level, than nonitemizers.

The deduction is seen as inviting the least amount of government involvement in influencing the direction of giving. And, finally, eliminating the deduction or replacing it with a tax credit or matching grant system would significantly shift giving away from several current recipient areas at a time when these areas are already undergoing severe economic strains.

B. Extending and Amplifying the Deduction

The Commission recognizes that the charitable deduction is used by fewer and fewer taxpayers—now fewer than one third—because of the liberalized standard deduction. So, to broaden the reach of the charitable deduction and to increase giving, the Commission recommends:

That all taxpayers who take the standard deduction should also be permitted to deduct charitable contributions as an additional, itemized deduction.

This extension of the deduction would, it is calculated, provide an inducement to give to nearly 60 million nonitemizers, and would thereby result in increased giving, according to econometric projections, of $1.9 billion in 1976 dollars.

This amount is still relatively modest in terms of the amount of giving that would be needed to restore giving to its level in 1960 before its decline in relative purchasing power set in—an increase in giving, in current dollars, of around $8 billion would be required. Moreover, while extending the deduction to nonitemizers would provide many millions of taxpayers with some inducement to give, the inducement would still be tied to the progressive rate structure of the income tax and would be markedly lower at low- and middle-income levels than it is at upper levels. Therefore, the Commission recommends as an additional new incentive for low- and middle-income contributors:

That families with incomes below $15,000 a year be allowed to *deduct twice the amount of their giving, and those with incomes between $15,000 and $30,000 be allowed to deduct 150 per cent of what they contribute.*

The "double deduction" and the 150 per cent deduction would have the effect of doubling the proportion of tax savings for charitable giving for low-income families and increasing the proportion by one half for middle-income families and would thus appreciably narrow the range in savings between these brackets and high-income taxpayers. The amount of giving induced and the efficiency of inducing it might, moreover, be impressive. According to econometric projections, $9.8 billion more in giving would be stimulated, at a cost of only $7.4 billion in tax revenue lost.

C. Increasing Corporate Giving

Corporate giving is still a relatively new element in American philanthropy; the corporate charitable deduction itself has been in effect only for forty years. And there are those on both the left and right who question whether corporations should be involved in philanthropy at all. While recognizing that such giving can only be a minor element in the corporation's role in society, the Commission also notes that only 20 per cent of corporate taxpayers in 1970 reported any charitable contributions and only 6 per cent made contributions of over $500. The record of corporate giving is an unimpressive and inadequate one, the Commission believes. Therefore, the Commission recommends:

That corporations set as a minimum goal, to be reached no later than 1980, the giving to charitable purposes of 2 per cent of pre-tax net income, and that further studies of means to stimulate corporate giving be pursued.

II. IMPROVING THE PHILANTHROPIC PROCESS

The social benefit that flows from giving and nonprofit activity results from a process of interaction—between donors and donees and between both and the society at large. In order to function properly—and to reassure a public grown skeptical of its institutions—this "philanthropic process" requires considerable openness between donors and donees and the public; it requires open minds as well as open doors. The tax-exempt status of nonprofit organizations, moreover, entails an obligation to openness, an accountability to the public for actions and expenditures.

Yet the Commission's research, including meetings with and reports from representatives of donee organizations, indicates that the process is operating imperfectly at best. So a number of recommendations were decided upon with the aim of improving the philanthropic process; the following are among the major ones. They fall into four categories: accountability, accessibility, personal or institutional self-benefiting, and influencing legislation.

A. Accountability

Demands for accountability that have been heard in the business and government worlds of late are also being sounded in the voluntary sector, reflecting the haphazard procedures for accountability that exist in the sector, the increasing use of public funds by nonprofit organizations, and the perception by some that private nonprofit organizations are too private. The Commission agrees that, with notable individual exceptions, the overall level of accountability in the voluntary sector is inadequate, and the Commission therefore recommends:

That all larger tax-exempt charitable organizations except churches and church affiliates be required to prepare and make readily available detailed annual reports on their finances, programs and priorities.

Annual reporting requirements that now apply to private foundations would, in effect, be extended to tax-exempt organizations with annual budgets of more than $100,000—including corporate giving programs but excluding religious organizations. These reports would have to be filed with appropriate state and federal agencies and be made readily available to interested parties upon request. Uniform accounting measures for comparable types of nonprofit organizations are recommended, and an accounting model is provided in the compen-

22

dium of Commission research, which is published separately.

That larger grant-making organizations be required to hold annual public meetings to discuss their programs, priorities and contributions.

This requirement would apply mainly to foundations, corporations and federated fund-raising groups such as United Ways, those with contribution budgets of $100,000 or more. Like the above requirement it would not apply to churches or church affiliates.

B. Accessibility

Greater accessibility by potential donees to donor institutions has frequently been espoused as a goal in the nonprofit sector, yet the evidence suggests that it has been a goal honored more in preachments than in practical pursuit. The Commission believes that greater accessibility can only enrich the philanthropic process, and it is concerned that because of insufficient accessibility, the process may not be fluid enough to respond to new needs. So, with the aim of encouraging and facilitating wider access to and greater venturesomeness by institutional philanthropy, the Commission recommends:

That legal responsibility for proper expenditure of foundation grants, now imposed on both foundations and recipients, be eliminated and that recipient organizations be made primarily responsible for their own expenditures.

The 1969 Tax Reform Act places on foundations and their officers "expenditure responsibility" for any grant that a foundation makes. This provision serves as a restraint on the openness and venturesomeness of foundations. It also puts foundations in a policing and surveillance role and thus undermines the autonomy of grantees. The provision creates both an unnecessary and undesirable duplication of responsibility, and should be repealed.

That tax-exempt organizations, particularly funding organizations, recognize an obligation to be responsive to changing viewpoints and emerging needs and that they take steps such as broadening their boards and staffs to insure that they are responsive.

23

All exempt organizations, especially those that serve to channel funds to other nonprofit groups, have a public obligation to be aware of and responsive to new attitudes and needs of all segments of society, and each organization should periodically broaden its board and staff if need be so that a wide range of viewpoints is reflected in the organization's governance and management.

The Commission rejects the notion that all voluntary organizations should be "representative" but observes that as more government funds flow into or through voluntary organizations they may have to consider inviting "public" members on their boards as an element of public access and control.

In addition to broadening existing organizations the Commission urges the establishment of new funding organizations and structural changes to broaden the spectrum of institutional philanthropy in general. An example is the "People's Trust" plan currently being explored in Atlanta; it would raise money in modest monthly pledges for projects close to the donors' homes.

C. Personal or Institutional Self-Benefiting

While tax-exempt charitable organizations are not allowed to make profits, situations have been uncovered in which personal money-making appeared to be the main purpose of the organization or of certain transactions made by the organization. Most notorious, perhaps, have been discoveries of instances where fund-raising and administrative costs have used as much as four out of every five dollars raised. The 1969 tax reform law placed stringent restrictions on self-benefiting by foundation personnel. The Commission believes that other tax-exempt organizations may be as open to such abuses, however, and it therefore favors extending the 1969 restriction to all exempt organizations, with appropriate modifications. Other remedies and restraints are considered desirable as well to insure public confidence that charitable nonprofit organizations do indeed serve only charitable nonprofit causes. The Commission recommends:

That all tax-exempt organizations be required to maintain "arms-length" business relationships with profit-making organiza-

tions or activities in which any principal of the exempt organization has a financial interest.

That a system of federal regulation be established for interstate charitable solicitations and that intrastate solicitations be more effectively regulated by state governments.

The Commission believes that the vast majority of charitable solicitations are conscientiously and economically undertaken. Nonetheless, cases of unduly costly or needless fund raising point to the absence of any focused mechanism for overseeing such activity and, if need be, applying sanctions. State regulation is weak and should be strengthened, but because many solicitations are spread over a number of states at once, federal regulation is needed.

The Commission recommends fuller disclosure requirements on solicitation costs and proposes that a special federal office be established to oversee solicitations and to take legal actions against improper, misleading or excessively costly fund raisings.

D. Influencing Legislation

Since 1934, organizations that are eligible to receive tax-deductible gifts have been prohibited from devoting a "substantial part" of their activities to "attempting to influence legislation."

Yet, since 1962, any business organization has been able to deduct costs of influencing legislation that affects the direct interest of the business. The anti-lobbying restriction operates unevenly among charitable groups themselves because of the vagueness that surrounds the term, "substantial part." Large organizations can lobby amply, smaller ones risk treading over some ill-defined line. Furthermore, constitutional questions are raised by what can be viewed as an infringement on free speech and on the right to petition government.

The Commission feels that the restriction inhibits a large and growing role of the voluntary sector. As government has expanded in relation to the nonprofit sector, the influencing of government has tended to become an ever more important function of nonprofit organizations. For many "public interest"

25

and "social action" groups, it is a principal means of furthering their causes. Therefore, the Commission recommends:

That nonprofit organizations, other than private foundations, be allowed the same freedom to attempt to influence legislation as are business corporations and trade associations, that toward this end Congress remove the current limitation on such activity by charitable groups eligible to receive tax-deductible gifts.

III. A PERMANENT COMMISSION

The Commission's studies have, it feels, significantly advanced the state of knowledge about America's third sector and its philanthropic underpinnings. Yet such is the immensity and diversity of this area of American life and such has been the scarcity of information that has faced the Commission that it inevitably has had to leave depths unfathomed.

A new organization of recognized national stature and authority is needed, the Commission believes, to further chart and study, and ultimately to strengthen the nonprofit sector and the practice of private giving for public purposes. In a time when the sector is subject to both economic strains and political and philosophical questioning, when profound changes are taking place in its role and relationship to government, and when philanthropy has failed to keep pace with society, in economic and financial terms at least, the Commission believes that such an entity is necessary for the growth, perhaps even the survival, of the sector as an effective instrument of individual initiative and social progress.

This Commission, in terminating its own work, puts forward as one of its major recommendations:

That a permanent national commission on the nonprofit sector be established by Congress.

Several major tasks of any new organization already await it. Among these is examining philanthropic priorities in light of America's changing social perceptions, of government's growing role in traditional philanthropic areas, and of the inevitably limited resources of private giving. Also, examining and advancing means of insulating voluntary organizations from the political and bureaucratic pressures that tend to accompany public funds.

Among other purposes and roles of the commission would be continuous collection of data on the sources and uses of the resources of the nonprofit sector; exploring and proposing ways of strengthening private giving and nonprofit activity; providing a forum for public discussion of issues affecting, and for commentary concerning, the nonprofit sector; studying the existing relationships between government and the nonprofit sector and acting as an ombudsman in protecting the interests of the sector as affected by government.

It is proposed that half the commission's membership be named by the President, subject to senatorial confirmation, the other half by the presidential appointees themselves. Funding for the commission would come half from government, half from private sources. The commission would be established as a permanent body, subject, of course, to periodic congressional review and the commission's demonstration of its benefit to society.

PART I

GIVING AND THE "THIRD SECTOR"

Findings of the Commission

I

THE THIRD SECTOR

On the map of American society, one of the least charted regions is variously known as the voluntary, the private non-profit or simply the third sector. Third, that is, after the often overshadowing worlds of government and business. While these two other realms have been and continue to be microscopically examined and analyzed and while their boundaries are for the most part readily identified by experts and laymen alike, the third sector—made up of nongovernmental, nonprofit associations and organizations—remains something of a terra incognita, barely explored in terms of its inner dynamics and motivations, and its social, economic and political relations to the rest of the world. As on ancient maps, its boundaries fade off into extensions of the imagination, and a monster or two may lurk in the surrounding seas.

Yet it is within this institutional domain that nearly all philanthropic input—giving and volunteering—is transformed into philanthropic output—goods and services for ultimate beneficiaries. So the Commission has attempted to take the measure of this area, both quantitatively and qualitatively, and has examined the sector's roles and rationales, past, present and future.

The sector as a whole is most broadly defined by what it is not. It is not government—that is, its component organizations do not command the full power and authority of government, although some may exercise powerful influences over their members and some may even perform certain functions of government. Educational accrediting organizations, for instance, exercise aspects of the governmental power of licensing. For that matter, political parties can be considered to be a part of this sector although their relationship to government is pervasive and in many cases—congressional party caucuses, for instance—inextricable.

On the other hand, the third sector is not business. Its orga-

31

nizations do not exist to make profit and those that enjoy tax immunities are specifically prohibited from doing so, although near the boundaries of the sector many groups do serve primarily the economic interests of their members. Chambers of commerce, labor unions, trade associations and the like hardly pretend to be principally altruistic.

The World of Philanthropy

Inside these negative boundaries is a somewhat narrower domain within which the world of philanthropy generally operates, a domain made up of private groups and institutions that are deemed to serve the public interest rather than a primarily self-benefiting one, and it is this narrower area that has been the principal focus of the Commission. This area is legally defined by laws that determine which types of organizations should be immune from income taxes and eligible to receive tax-deductible contributions from individuals and corporations. Under the Internal Revenue Code, twenty categories of organizations are exempt from federal income tax, but most of those that are eligible to receive tax-deductible gifts as well fall in one category of the code, Section 501(c)(3). To qualify for exemption under this section, whose "501(c)(3)" designation has become for the nonprofit world virtually synonymous with tax deductibility, an organization must operate exclusively for one or more of these broad purposes: charitable, religious, scientific, literary, educational. Two narrower aims are specified as well: testing for public safety and prevention of cruelty to children or animals. The code further states that no "substantial" part of such an organization's activities may be devoted to attempting to influence legislation and that the organization may not participate at all in candidates' political campaigns.

But even these boundaries, though narrower than those set by the nongovernment, nonprofit definition, are immensely broad and vague. What is charitable, what educational, what religious? In a time in which new and unconventional religious sects are being born, it seems, almost monthly, which are genuine expressions of the religious impulse that are legitimately protected from both taxes and governmental scrutiny? Which are essentially secular cults, which outright frauds? The Internal Revenue Service, for one, wishes it had an all-purpose definition of religion to work with. When is an activity educational rather than primarily propagandistic (and thus barred from tax-deductible gifts under the current law)? Considerable litigation and administrative judgement has been devoted to answering such questions. Philosophical as well as legal arguments can be and are raised, moreover, as to whether whole groups of organizations within the tax-exempt categories are truly oriented to the public interest—their justification for tax privilege—or whether they serve primarily to further the interests of a select group.

The Commission has not attempted to establish a definition or principle by which nonprofit, nongovernmental organizations can be judged to be in the public interest and thus a proper concern of and channel for philanthropy. Others have tried to form such a definition, but none has unquestionably succeeded. In any case, a certain flexibility is seen as desirable, both philosophically and legally, in defining the public interest. One of the main virtues of the private nonprofit sector lies in its very testing and extension of any definition of the public interest, so it would be counter-productive to try to establish boundaries in more than a general, expandable sense. Similarly, although this Commission has operated under the rubric of "public needs," no attempt has been made to catalogue, let alone establish any priority scale of, such needs.* Like the public interest, the closely related concept of public needs is itself fluid and shifting. A constant and transcendent public need by which the voluntary sector and philanthropy may perhaps be ultimately judged is how effectively they keep abreast of this shifting and how well they are deemed to meet whatever new public needs are perceived.

Likewise, no attempt has been made to attach, and certainly none has succeeded in attaching, a new, better name to the territory under examination, even though none of the existing names is universally admired. Here, and throughout the report, the terms voluntary sector, private nonprofit sector (or simply

*See comment by GRACIELA OLIVAREZ, page 197.

33

nonprofit sector for short) or third sector are used interchangeably and in all cases except where otherwise indicated are
meant to exclude organizations that primarily serve the interests of their own members.

Dimensions of the Voluntary Sector

What are the dimensions of this sector? To the extent that
they have been measured at all, the measurement has usually
been only a partial one that looks at the amount of private
giving and volunteer activity that goes into nonprofit organizations. Even on this incomplete scale, however, it is clear that
the nonprofit sector accounts for a very large amount of time
and money. According to estimates based on surveys made for
the Commission, which are described more fully in the next
chapter, at least $25 billion annually is given to various causes
and organizations, and an equal amount worth of volunteer
work is devoted to philanthropic activity. Yet these figures
require some subtraction, and a good deal of addition. For one,
a small but significant and growing amount of private giving
goes to public institutions, mainly state colleges and universities. On the other hand, a sizable share of the funding of the
nonprofit sector comes from the government nowadays, and
considerable additional funds come from endowment and other
investment income and from operating revenues, including
payments to nonprofit organizations by those who use their
services—students' tuitions, medical patients' fees and the like.
Government funding, endowment income and service charges
must be added to the overall ledger of the voluntary sector.
When they are, a rough extrapolation from available data indicates the total annual receipts of the private nonprofit sector to
be in the range of $80 billion, or half as much as Americans
spend on food in a year. Here is an approximate breakdown,
again based on rough estimations, of what the major areas
within the nonprofit sector receive and spend. (Only money
inputs are indicated; volunteer work, free corporate services
and the like are not included.)

34

REVENUES OF THE VOLUNTARY SECTOR

Estimates of Amounts of Private and Government Funds Received by Private Nonprofit Organizations in Major Recipient Areas, 1974

(In billions of dollars)

	PRIVATE FUNDS			GOVERN- MENT FUNDS	TOTAL
	Philan- thropy	Service Charges and Endowment Income	Total		
Health	$4.0	$17.8	$21.8	$15.7	$37.5
Education	4.2	7.5	11.7	1.6	13.3
Other (Welfare, Culture, etc.)	5.4	6.0	11.4	5.9	17.3
Total (except Religion)	$13.6	$31.3	$44.9	$23.2	$68.1
Religion	11.7	0.8	12.5	—	12.5
Grand Total	$25.3	$32.1	$57.4	$23.2	$80.6

Source: Commission on Private
Philanthropy and
Public Needs

Another measure of the dimensions of the nonprofit sector is the employment it accounts for. Approximately 4.6 million wage and salary workers are estimated to have worked in the nonprofit sector in 1974, or 5.2 per cent of the total American workforce for that year. One out of every ten service workers in the United States is employed by a nonprofit organization. The proportion of professional workers is even higher—nearly one out of six.

For a physical count of nonprofit organizations, the Commission has turned to a number of sources. The Internal Revenue Service lists, as of June, 1975, 691,627 exempt organizations, groups that have formally filed for and been accorded exemption from federal income taxes. But that number does not include a great many church organizations which automatically enjoy exemption from federal income taxes without filing, nor does it include numerous small organizations that never feel the need to file for tax exemption. On the other hand, it does include a large number of groups that fall outside the philanthropic part of the nonprofit sector, such as labor unions and fraternal organizations, and it also counts a good many groups that are only active for a short time. One Commission report calculates that a "core group" of traditional philanthropic organizations includes 350,000 religious organizations, 37,000 human service organizations, 6,000 museums, 5,500 private libraries, 4,600 privately supported secondary schools, 3,500 private hospitals, 1,514 private institutions of higher education, and 1,100 symphony orchestras. Some other recent calculations: There are 1,000 national professional associations. New York City alone has around 6,000 block associations. And a study of voluntary groups in the town of Arlington, Mass., identified some 350 such groups there, serving a population of around 52,000. This last finding confirms earlier estimates of proportions between community size and the number of voluntary groups, and gives support to the extrapolation that in all, counting local chapters of regional or national groups, there may be as many as six million private voluntary organizations in the United States. A purely intuitive indication that this very large number is feasible can be glimpsed in a minute sample of nonprofit groups. To name a few:

Bedford-Stuyvesant Restoration Corporation, Phillips Exeter Academy, American Acupuncture and Herbs Research Institute, Senior Citizens Association of Wausau (Wisc.), Talmudic Research Institute, New Alchemy Institute, Aspen Institute for Humanistic Studies, Chapin School Ltd., Citizens Committee on Modernization of Maryland Courts and Justice, Bethlehem (Pa.) Public Library, Visiting Nurse Association of Milwaukee, YMCA Railroad Branch of Toledo, Chinatown (N.Y.) Day Care Center, Zen Center of Los Angeles, Big Brothers of Rapid City, World Affairs Council of Syracuse, N.Y., American Parkinson Disease Association, Bethel Temple of Evansville (Ind.),

Metropolitan Opera Company, Fathers Club of Mt. St. Mary's Academy (Watchung, N.J.), Mothers Club of Stanford University, Sons and Daughters of Idaho Pioneers, Family Planning Committee of Greater Fall River (Mass.).

Ultimate Beneficiaries

The arithmetic of the nonprofit sector finds much of its significance in less quantifiable and even less precise dimensions—in the human measurements of who is served, who is affected by nonprofit groups and activities. In some sense, everybody is: the contributions of voluntary organizations to broadscale social and scientific advances have been widely and frequently extolled. Charitable groups were in the forefront of ridding society of child labor, abolitionist groups in tearing down the institution of slavery, civic-minded groups in purging the spoils system from public office. The benefits of nonprofit scientific and technological research include the great reduction of scourges such as tuberculosis and polio, malaria, typhus, influenza, rabies, yaws, bilharziasis, syphilis and amoebic dysentery. These are among the myriad products of the nonprofit sector that have at least indirectly affected all Americans and much of the rest of the world besides.

Perhaps the nonprofit activity that most directly touches the lives of most Americans today is noncommercial "public" television. A bare concept twenty-five years ago, its development was underwritten mainly by foundations. Today it comprises a network of some 240 stations valued at billions of dollars, is increasingly supported by small, "subscriber" contributions and has broadened and enriched a medium that occupies hours of the average American's day.

More particularly benefited by voluntary organizations are the one quarter of all college and university students who attend private institutions of higher education. For hundreds of millions of Americans, private community hospitals, accounting for half of all hospitals in the United States, have been, as one Commission study puts it, "the primary site for handling the most dramatic of human experiences—birth, death, and the

37

alleviation of personal suffering." In this secular age, too, it is worth noting that the largest category in the nonprofit sector is still very large indeed, that nearly two out of three Americans belong to and evidently find comfort and inspiration in the nation's hundreds of thousands of religious organizations. All told, it would be hard to imagine American life without voluntary nonprofit organizations and associations, so entwined are they in the very fabric of our society, from massive national organizations to the local Girl Scouts, the parent-teachers association or the bottle-recycling group.

Government and Voluntary Association

Ultimately, the nonprofit sector's significance, and any measure of its continuing importance, lies in its broader societal role, as seen in the long history of voluntary association and in what signs can currently be glimpsed of new or continuing directions. To talk of the sector's role in society inevitably means looking at voluntary activity and association alongside of government. Both are expressions of the same disposition of people to join together to achieve a common end, and in much of the United States' experience they have been complementary expressions. But in global terms they often have functioned and do function as mutually competitive forces. No government tolerates all forms of voluntary association; groups that are seen as threatening a country's security or that pursue common criminal purposes are routinely suppressed. The tensions between voluntary association and government run broader and deeper in many parts of the world, however, and have done so through many periods of history.

Sociologist Robert A. Nisbet has written of the "momentous conflicts of jurisdiction between the political state and the social associations lying intermediate to it and the individual." These have been, he writes, "of all the conflicts in history, the most fateful." Such conflicts can be traced at least as far back as democratic Greece and imperial Rome, in both of which societies governments were at times hostile to voluntary association. Imperial Rome, wrote Gibbon, "viewed with the utmost jealousy and distrust any association among its subjects."

The Middle Ages witnessed a flourishing in Europe of more or less autonomous groupings—guilds, churches, fiefdoms—within weak central governments. But modern history can be seen at least in part as being patterned by the return to Greek and Roman affinities for the central, dominant state, with an accompanying discouragement of nongovernmental groups. The foremost philosophers of this monism of the state in modern times were Thomas Hobbes and Jean Jacques Rousseau, and the French Revolution was one of its most exuberant expressions. Charitable, literary, educational and cultural societies were banned in the brittle course of the revolution. "A state that is truly free," declared a legislator of revolutionary France, "ought not to suffer within its bosom any association, not even such as, being dedicated to public improvement, has merited well of the country."

"Americans Are Forever Forming Associations"

In spite of this inhospitable historical and philosophical setting, "association dedicated to public improvement" found fertile territory in the New World, a land colonized far from the reach of central governments, a vast land that did not lend itself well to strong central government of its own and in frontier areas was slow to adopt even minimal local governments. As historian Daniel Boorstin has observed, America evidenced a profound tendency to rely on voluntary, nongovernmental organizations and associations to pursue community purposes "from the beginning." As this country was settled, he writes, "communities existed before governments were there to care for public needs." The result was that "voluntary collaborative activities" were set up first to provide basic social services. Government followed later on.

It is no historical accident that one of the Founding Fathers is nearly as famous for his development of nongovernmental means to public ends as he is for his role in shaping and representing the fledgling republic. Benjamin Franklin's institutings outside of government compose a major portion of the

39

index of the voluntary sector. He was the leading force in founding a library, a volunteer fire department, a hospital, a university and a research institution. An historical survey of philanthropy made for the Commission notes: "Franklin did not invent the principle of improving social conditions through voluntary association, but more than any American before him he showed the availability, usefulness and appropriateness to American conditions."

"The principle of voluntary association accorded so well with American political and economic theories," the survey observes further, "that as early as 1820 the larger cities had an embarrassment of benevolent organizations." Fifteen years later, this propensity to organize became the subject of one of Alexis de Tocqueville's most famous of many famous observations about the new nation:

"Americans of all ages, all stations in life, and all types of disposition are forever forming associations. There are not only commercial and industrial associations in which all take part, but others of a thousand different types—religious, moral, serious, futile, very general and very limited, immensely large and very minute. Americans combine to give fetes, found seminaries, build churches, distribute books and send missionaries to the antipodes. Hospitals, prisons and schools take shape that way. Finally, if they want to proclaim a truth or propagate some feeling by the encouragement of a great example, they form an association. In every case, at the head of any new undertaking, where in France you would find the government or in England some territorial magnate, in the United States you are sure to find an association."

Evolutions Within the Third Sector

This observation applies to the United States almost as fully 140 years later. Today, in fact, private association appears to be so deeply embedded and to exist on so much broader a scale in the United States than in other parts of the world as to represent one of the principal distinguishing characteristics of American society. Yet the purposes of voluntary organization have hardly remained stationary or of the same relative significance within the voluntary sector over the years.

In a pattern of evolution that has repeated itself in different areas of society, government has taken over many services and functions of the nonprofit sector, and new focuses of nonprofit activity and organization have emerged (a process that is described further in Chapter IV). Schools, as de Tocqueville observed, were generally founded and run by nongovernmental organizations, often churches, in early America. But soon after de Tocqueville's observations were published in 1835, the public school system began to take hold in the United States, and today only one out of ten primary and secondary school students goes to nonpublic schools. Higher education and aid to the poor correspondingly accounted for more and more nonprofit activity as the nineteenth century progressed. Then, beginning in the late nineteenth century, many of today's giant state universities got their start, and public institutions began to challenge the primacy of private institutions in higher education as well. The private nonprofit sector was the chief dispenser of "charity" well into this century, but in recent decades this function has increasingly been absorbed by government welfare and social insurance programs.

Today we appear to be on the threshold of yet another major expansion by government in an area that until a few years ago was dominated by private nonprofit (and profit) organizations, the health field. A Commission study of philanthropy in this area anticipates that by the mid-1980's, more than half of all spending on health in the United States will be accounted for by government programs, with much of the rest flowing through government-regulated private insurance plans.

Underlying Functions of Voluntary Groups

The end purposes of nonprofit activity have changed considerably over the course of American history, therefore, and unquestionably will continue to change. Yet certain basic functions—underlying social roles that have been characteristic of much or all nonprofit activity regardless of the particular ser-

41

vice or cause involved—have endured throughout the changes that have taken place. This is not to say, of course, that all nonprofit organizations are performing these functions optimally or even adequately. Indeed, as described in Chapter VII of this report, expert research the Commission has received and informal testimony it has listened to suggest that many organizations in the sector fall well short of their capabilities. Yet the same research and testimony is virtually unanimous in finding distinctive functions for the nonprofit sector and in asserting that these functions are today as important as they ever have been to the health and progress of American society, more important in some cases than ever. Among these basic functions are the following:

—*Initiating new ideas and processes.* ". . . There are critical reasons for maintaining a vital balance of public and private support for human services," asserts a Commission report by Wilbur J. Cohen, former Secretary of Health, Education and Welfare, "not the least of which is the continuing task of innovating in areas where public agencies lack knowledge or are afraid to venture. . . .The private sector is adept at innovation, and at providing the models government needs."

"A new idea stands a better chance of survival in a social system with many kinds of initiative and decision," observes a Commission study of the health field. Government undoubtedly provides the most fertile arena for certain kinds of initiative and innovation, but certain new ideas, these and other Commission reports indicate, stand a better chance of survival and growth in the nonprofit sector than in the corridors of government.

"The development of the early types of both health maintenance organizations and the physicians' assistance [paramedical aides] programs would never have surfaced if they had required prior public sector consensus and support," says the Commission's health study. Another study—on the role of philanthropy in the environmental field—finds: "The perspective of governmental agencies, even in the research-only . . . agencies. . ., tends to be limited and dominated by existing and agency views of the problems and alternative strategies for 'solving' the problem . . . It is difficult to induce . . . governmental agencies

42

. . . to undertake new directions of research and analysis." The "pioneering" role of nonprofit organizations has long been recognized. More than half a century ago, Beatrice and Sidney Webb, writing on the "Sphere of Voluntary Agencies," found these agencies capable of "many kinds . . . of . . . treatment . . . the public authorities are not likely themselves to initiate." Nongovernmental organizations, precisely because they are nongovernmental and need not be attuned to a broad and diverse constituency, can take chances, experiment in areas where legislators and government agencies are hesitant to tread.

Once successfully pioneered by nonprofit groups, and having established their legitimacy and worthiness, new ideas and processes can be, and often have been, supported and expanded by government. Birth-control technology, to take a relatively recent example, was pioneered by the nonprofit world in its more controversial beginnings and today is heavily underwritten by many governments throughout the world.

—*Developing public policy.* Standing outside of government, voluntary organizations not only can try out new ideas, initiate services, that may be too controversial for government bodies to deal with at early stages, but can exercise a direct influence on shaping and advancing government policy in broad areas in which the government is already involved. Groups specializing in certain policy areas are continually producing research and analysis, information and viewpoints, especially on long-range policy matters, that may be lacking at times in government circles themselves, preoccupied as they often are with day-to-day operating concerns. A major function of nonprofit groups in public policy development has been to help clarify and define issues for public consideration, both at local and regional levels, as the Regional Plan Association does through its studies and proposals for the New York metropolitan area, or as The Brookings Institution does at the national level. Privately sponsored special commissions and boards of inquiry have been frequently formed at both levels to focus analysis and attention on issues as diverse as hunger, cable communication and legalized gambling.

—*Supporting minority or local interests.* For many of the same

43

reasons the nonprofit world can experiment with new ideas less cautiously than government, voluntary groups can support causes and interests that may be swept aside by majoritarian priorities or prejudices. The civil rights movement grew out of the initiatives of nonprofit organizations such as the NAACP; the consumer and environmental movements, once the concerns of only a few perceptive or single-minded people, also found their early nourishment in private groups. But the causes need not be—or may not ever come to be regarded as—so large and socially significant. William S. Vickrey, an economist at Columbia University, has written of the "cumbersomeness of public agencies in dealing with relatively small-scale activities," of the impediments facing "high-level decision-making bodies on matters of small magnitude in which they have relatively little basis for judgment." More specialized private agencies may be able to operate efficiently and intelligently within their spheres, may be more sensitive to small-scale problems than government. In the health field, for example, a Commission report notes that nonprofit organizations "can assist in support of health programs for religious and ethnic groups, migratory workers, and racial minority groups which the public sector cannot often address . . . Private philanthropy will be needed in the future to even out some of the inequities which will invariably occur beween different communities, and to respond to the health needs of groups too culturally different to gain adequate public support."

—*Providing services that the government is constitutionally barred from providing.* In the United States, the government is proscribed from entering the broadest area of the nonprofit sector, religion. So there is simply no alternative to the nonprofit sector if religious functions are to be filled at all in this country. Similarly, as the Council on Foundations points out in its report to the Commission, the establishment in 1973 of a private nonprofit National News Council to oversee the news media "is an experiment that, if not totally off-limits to the government because of the First Amendment, is clearly not the kind of function that it should or would undertake."

—*Overseeing government.* Alongside government's constitutional inhibitions are its institutional ones. Despite its own

44

internal checks and balances, government can hardly be counted on to keep a disinterested eye on itself. In his historical
perspective on philanthropy written for the Commission, historian Robert H. Bremner observes: "A marked tendency of
American philanthropy has been to encourage, assist and even
goad democratic government—and democratic citizens—toward
better performance of civic duties and closer attention to social
requirements." The Nathan Committee, which looked at philanthropy in Great Britain a quarter century ago, saw much
the same role for voluntary groups. "They are able to stand
aside from and criticize state action, or inaction, in the interests of the inarticulate man-in-the-street." As government's role
in many areas formerly dominated by nongovernmental groups
grows ever larger, and the voluntary role grows correspondingly smaller, the monitoring and influencing of government may
be emerging as one of the single most important and effective
functions of the private nonprofit sector.

—Overseeing the market place. While most of the third sector's
activity relates more closely to government than to the business
sector because of the nonprofit, public-interest common de-
nominator of government and voluntary organizations, the sector does play a role, and perhaps a growing one, in relation to
the business world. In some areas, voluntary organizations provide a direct alternative to, and a kind of yardstick for, business organizations. Nonprofit hospitals and research organizations, for instance, operate in competition with close commercial counterparts. A number of nonprofit groups make it their
business to keep a critical gaze on business, including labor
union activity, as well. Potentially freer from the influence of
powerful economic interests, nonprofit groups can act as de-
tached overseers of the market place in ways that government
agencies and legislators are often restrained from doing.

—Bringing the sectors together. Nonprofit organizations frequently serve to stimulate and coordinate activities in which
government or business or both interact with voluntary groups
to pursue public purposes. Organization for community development is one example of this synergistic role. Another is the
practice by a group such as The Nature Conservancy of enlist-
ing the help of industry in the form of low-interest loans to buy

45

land for preservation and conservation purposes, land that may eventually be turned over to government ownership. The fact that voluntary organizations have neither commercial interests to pursue nor official status often makes them best suited to act as intermediary or coordinator in activities involving government and business.

—*Giving aid abroad.* In a time of heightened nationalistic sensitivities, especially where official American actions abroad are concerned, nonprofit organizations have been able to offer aid in situations where government help would be politically unacceptable. Workers for the American Friends Service Committee, for instance, were able to remain behind in Da Nang during the North Vietnamese takeover of that city and were able to help war victims there even though the United States government was considered hostile by the city's occupiers. As a Ford Foundation annual report observed a few years ago: ". . . Our welcome in sensitive areas often derives from the fact that we are not a government."

—*Furthering active citizenship and altruism.* While the previous categories deal mainly with the important roles nonprofit organizations serve for the society as a whole or for certain beneficiary segments of the society, one of the broadest and most important functions voluntary groups perform derives not so much from what they do for beneficiaries as what they do for participants. Voluntary groups serve as ready and accessible outlets for public-spirited initiative and activity—for philanthropy broadly defined. In a complex urbanized and suburbanized society, the individual acting alone can hope to make little impress on community or national problems, is often at a loss to find and help those who need help. Many government agencies have highly structured work arrangements and cannot or do not readily receive the assistance of public-spirited citizens. But those so minded can usually join or can help form a voluntary organization as an effective vehicle for altruistic action, and this possibility itself serves as a constant encouragement to altruism, to an active involvement in public causes, which is of the very essence in a healthy democratic society.

46

New Frontiers and an Ageless Rationale

These vital roles for voluntary organizations continue to serve and influence areas of society that have traditonally been the concern of the nonprofit sector. In addition, many new or greatly expanded concerns of voluntary activity have emerged in recent years as challenging new frontiers of the sector and of its particular capabilities. "Over the past 20 years," observes Pablo Eisenberg, head of the Center for Community Change, "hundreds if not thousands of new local organizations have been created to deal with issues such as ecology, consumer problems, economic and social self-determination, public-interest law, poverty and neighborhood revitalization . . . groups with different purposes and structures and, in some cases, constituencies." Indeed, a recent survey indicates that possibly as many as 40,000 environmental organizations alone have sprung up throughout the country, mostly in the last few years. And in a Commission study of philanthropy in five cities, one major conclusion is that "nonprofit, tax-exempt organizations continue to grow in each of the cities studied."

For all the absorptions by government and despite severe financial difficulties of many voluntary organizations—related developments that are discussed in later chapters—it would appear, in other words, that the impulse to associate is still very strong. Indeed, there are social currents in motion that should be adding fresh impetus and vitality to this ageless expression of man's community with man.

One current is the sense of alienation that modern men and women are widely viewed as experiencing in the face of giant, impersonal institutions of government and business. The generally smaller size and more perceptible humanity of voluntary groups—be they block associations, local chapters of the American Legion or women's rights organizations—would appear to offer at least a partial antidote to any contemporary malaise stemming from feelings of ineffectiveness or unidentity. As Richard W. Lyman, president of Stanford University, wrote recently in an essay entitled "In Defense of the Private Sector," "People everywhere are yearning for the chance to feel significant as individuals. They are yearning for institutions built on

47

a human scale, and responsive to human needs and aspirations. Is this not precisely what we have believed in and worked for, long before it became so popular to do so?"

In addition to responding to an existential yearning, the voluntary sector should appeal more than ever today in terms of its bedrock grounding in the spirit and political philosophy of pluralism—in the idea that society benefits from having many different ways for striving to advance the common weal. The federal government's unavailing efforts to control the economy follow many frustrating social programs of the Great Society and both add to the evidence of our senses that in our increasingly complex society there is no one body, one governing structure, that holds the answers to society's problems, is equipped to find the answers by itself or could put them into effect if it did. In the wake of Watergate, moreoever, we are probably less persuaded than ever to stake our destiny totally on the wisdom or beneficence of centralized authority. This sorry and sordid chapter in recent history has dramatically demonstrated the virtues of diffusion of power and decentralization of decision making in public affairs, and it has demonstrated the correlative virtues of a vigorous public-minded and independent sector. The sector ideally should not compete with government so much as complement it and help humanize it, however. Nor because of institutional inertia or self-protectiveness should it or parts of it stand in the way of proper extensions of government into areas where, because of the demands of scale or equity, the private sector simply cannot fill a collective want. The sector should not be at odds with government, in other words, so much as outside of it and in addition to it.

In furtherance of its own role of serving the public interest, government at the same time should actively encourage a large and vigorous voluntary sector that can help carry the burdens of public services. For to operate effectively, and humanely, government must take care not to overload its own mechanisms by attempting to bring every public purpose directly under its direction and control.

The late Walter Lippmann recognized this central importance to government, and to American society at large, of nongovernmental organization. American democracy, he wrote a number of years ago, "has worked, I am convinced, for two reasons. The first is that government in America has not, hitherto, been permitted to attempt to do too many things; its problems have been kept within the capacity of ordinary men. The second . . . is that outside the government and outside the party system, there have existed independent institutions and independent men . . ." His observation describes the ultimate rationale for a "third" sector in American society, a rationale that applies as fully for today and tomorrow as it did for yesterday.

Sources for Chapter I

William D. Andrews, "Personal Deductions in an Ideal Income Tax," *Harvard Law Review*, Vol. 86, No. 2, December 1972.

Robert J. Blendon, *The Changing Role of Private Philanthropy in Health Affairs.**

Blair T. Bower, *The Role of Private Philanthropy in Relation to Environment—Pollution.**

Robert H. Bremner, *Private Philanthropy and Public Needs: An Historical Perspective.**

John J. Carson and Harry V. Hodson, eds., *Philanthropy in the '70's: An Anglo-American Discussion*, Council on Foundations, Inc., New York, 1973.

Earl F. Cheit and Theodore E. Lobman III, *Private Philanthropy and Higher Education.**

Coalition for the Public Good Thru Voluntary Initiative, *Statement Prepared for the Commission on Private Philanthropy and Public Needs.**

Wilbur J. Cohen, *Some Aspects of Evolving Social Policy in Relation to Private Philanthropy.**

Commission on Foundations and Private Philanthropy, *Foundations, Private Giving and Public Policy*, University of Chicago Press, Chicago, 1970.

Committee on the Law and Practice Relating to Charitable Trusts (Nathan Committee), *Report on Charitable Trusts,* Her Majesty's Stationery Office, London, 1952.

Council on Foundations, Inc., *Private Foundations and the 1969 Tax Reform Act.**

Fred R. Crawford, *Non-Economic Motivational Factors in Philanthropic Behavior.**

Pablo Eisenberg, "The Filer Commission: A Critical Perspective," in *The Grantsmanship Center News*, Vol. 2, No. 1, December, 1974-January, 1975.

Donald A. Erickson, *Philanthropy, Public Needs and Nonpublic Schools.**

Solomon Fabricant, *Philanthropy in the American Economy*, Foundation News, Vol. X, No. 5. September-October, 1969.

Caryl P. Haskins, *The Role of Private Philanthropy and Public Support of Science in the United States.**

Hans H. Jenny, *Philanthropy in Higher Education.**

Janet Koch, *The Role of Philanthropy in the Environmental Field—Preservation of Natural Lands and Historic Properties.**

Robert L. Lamborn, Cary Potter, Al H. Senske, *The Nonpublic School and Private Philanthropy.**

Richard W. Lyman, "In Defense of the Private Sector," *Daedalus*, Winter, 1975.

William G. McLoughlin, "Changing Patterns of Protestant Philanthropy 1607-1969," in *The Religious Situation*, Beacon Press, Boston, 1969.

National Center for Voluntary Action, *A Report on Voluntary Activities and Leadership Opinion.**

Robert A. Nisbet, *Community and Power*, Oxford University Press, New York, 1962.

David Owen, *English Philanthropy, 1660-1960*, Harvard University Press, Cambridge, 1964.

Gabriel G. Rudney, *Scope of the Private Voluntary Charitable Sector, 1974.**

John F. Shannon and L. Richard Gabler, *The Exemption of Religious, Educational and Charitable Institutions from Property Taxation.**

David Horton Smith and Burt R. Baldwin, "Voluntary Association and Volunteering in the United States," in *Voluntary Action Research 1974*, D.C. Heath and Company, Boston, 1975.

Lawrence M. Stone, *The Charitable Foundation: Its Governance.**

T. Nicolaus Tideman, *Employment and Earnings in the Non-Profit Charitable Sector.**

United States Senate, Report of Proceedings, Subcommittee on Foundations, Committee on Finance, *The Role of Foundations Today and the Effect of the Tax Reform Act of 1969 Upon Foundations*, October 1 and 2, 1973.

United States Senate, Report of Proceedings, Subcommittee on Foundations, Committee on Finance, *Impact of Current Economic Crisis on Funds and Recipients of Foundation Money*, November 25, 1974.

Joseph L. Vigilante and Ruth Kantrow, *The Voluntary Social Agency Experiments, Innovates, Demonstrates, and Influences Public Social Policy: The Community Service Society of New York 1930-1970.**

Burton A. Weisbrod, *The Size of the Voluntary Nonprofit Sector: Concepts and Measures.**

Burton A. Weisbrod, "Toward A Theory of the Voluntary Non-Profit Sector in a Three-Sector Economy," in *Altruism, Morality and Economic Theory*, Edmund S. Phelps, Ed., Russell Sage Foundation, New York, 1975.

Laurens Williams and Donald V. Moorehead, *An Analysis of the Federal Tax Distinctions Between Public and Private Charitable Organizations.**

Ellen Winston, *Some Aspects of Private Philanthropy in Relation to Social Welfare.**

Adam Yarmolinsky, *The Tax Legislative Process and the Appropriations Process.**

Adam Yarmolinsky, *Philanthropic Activity in International Affairs.**

Paul N. Ylvisaker and Jane H. Mavity, *The Role of Private Philanthropy in Public Affairs.**

*Denotes reports and studies undertaken for the Commission.

II

PRIVATE GIVING FOR
PUBLIC PURPOSES

The spirit of private giving for public purposes has been the object of immeasurable exhortation and applause and also a great deal of cynicism. It has been praised as embodying humankind's noblest instincts—generosity, altruism, benevolent initiative—and disdained for reflecting some of our most ignoble—paternalism, elitism, egotism. It has been espoused in terms of transcendent religious principles and found wanting by the standards of secular theologies, the catechisms of democracy and egalitarianism.

Yet whatever disagreements in viewpoint may surround the personal motivations and social effects of giving, there is little question that an important institutional area of American life —the private nonprofit sector—could not exist without it. Private support is a fundamental underpinning for hundreds of thousands of institutions and organizations; it is the ingredient that keeps private nonprofit organizations alive and private, keeps them from withering away or becoming mere adjuncts of government. And it is, without question, a very sizable ingredient.

Sizes, Sources and Destinations of Giving

"Private giving for public purposes" is a cumbersome phrase for what this ingredient, this chapter and a good part of the Commission's concern has been about. "Philanthropy" is an easier term to use, but in these socially sensitive times it probably rings, in many ears, of noblesse oblige and may have as many negative as positive overtones. So may "charity." But by any name—and this report uses all of them somewhat loosely and interchangeably—private giving for public purposes is a large

53

WHOM THE GIVING COMES FROM

Shares of Giving and Percentages of all Households,
by 1973 total household income

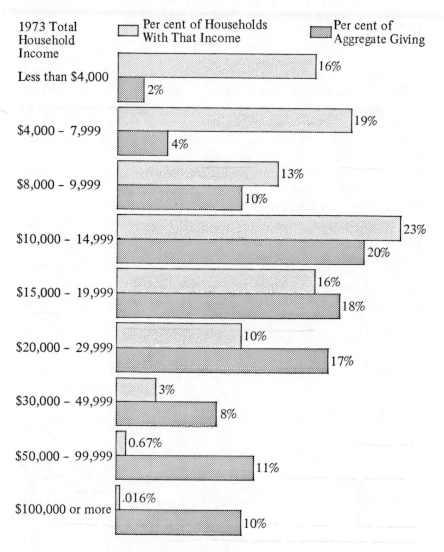

Source: University of Michigan–U.S. Census Bureau Survey
for Commission on Private Philanthropy and Public Needs

and influential factor in American society in terms of raw economic measurements alone.

A national sample survey on giving behavior and attitudes was conducted for the Commission by the Survey Research Center of the Institute for Social Research at the University of Michigan working in conjunction with the U.S. Census Bureau. Some 2,917 heads of households were questioned at length, and from the responses it is projected that philanthropic giving by individuals may come to as much as $26 billion a year (as of 1973).* The survey figures refer to contributions by living individuals only, which make up by far the largest source of philanthropic funds, accounting for about 79 per cent of all giving in 1974. In addition, answers to questions about volunteer time and the dollar value of such time indicate that nearly six billion womanhours and manhours are contributed annually to philanthropic activity in the United States, at a value of around $26 billion. The other major categories of giving and estimates of the amounts of each during 1974 are: bequests ($2.07 billion), foundations ($2.11 billion), and corporations ($1.25 billion in direct dollar contributions alone, not including below-market-rate loans, providing of corporate facilities and services and other frequently contributed non-cash benefits). All told, private giving for public purposes appears to add up to $50 billion or more a year in money and services, or more than half of what is spent each year on national defense.

Who gives how much to what? A major area of interest to the Commission in relation to public policy questions has been precisely from whom philanthropic giving comes and where it goes. The University of Michigan-Census Bureau survey affirmed that giving is by no means a homogeneous process.

*The measurement of giving is still more art than science, and estimates vary as do bases for making them. National giving aggregates indicated by the Commission's sample survey are projected from respondents' own assessments of their giving and of their income levels. Other estimates of national giving levels are based on tax deductions claimed for giving plus extrapolations for giving that is not deducted. The Commission's survey estimate of $26 billion for individual giving in 1973 is higher than other major reckonings, which range from $18 billion to $23 billion. One major difference between the survey's findings and that of other giving estimates lies in projections of the amount of giving at upper income levels, which the Commission's survey finds to account for a larger absolute amount and larger share of overall giving than do other estimates, in part, perhaps, because some respondents may both overstate their giving and understate their income.

Among the findings is that the level of giving goes up with the level of education: a college graduate gives six times as much as someone with only a grade-school education ($924 compared to $162 in average annual giving). And even when factors such as higher income, which tends to accompany a higher education, are discounted the giving of a college graduate is three times that of a grade school graduate. "Giving can . . . be expected to depend on education for a variety of reasons," observes the survey report, "ranging from the greater income-security and stability of the well-educated to their greater feeling of social responsibility (or debt to society)." The survey also shows that the old give more than the young: average annual giving for someone in the 18 to 24-year-old range was $60 compared to $742 for someone 75 or older. "The pessimistic interpretation would be that each new 'younger' generation is less altruistic than the previous one," says the survey report, "or that the proximity of eternal judgement motivates the aged. But people may have fewer economic responsibilities and uncertainties as they get older and more assets and accumulated rights."

Other findings are that the married give more than the single, small town residents more than city dwellers, the religious more than the unreligious and, least surprising but most determinant of all, the rich more than the unrich. The survey finds that a disproportionate amount of philanthropic giving comes from the highest income levels—some 21 per cent of individual giving from the less than 1 per cent of households with incomes above $50,000 a year. (See footnote on page 55. Other estimates of giving are less top-heavy but still attribute as much as 13 per cent of individual giving to households with incomes above $50,000.) But the survey also indicates that most giving comes from low- and middle-income ranks—54 per cent from the 87 per cent of households with incomes below $20,000.

The survey finds that the giving of time, in the form of volunteer work, correlates closely with the giving of money, that those who give one are likely to give the other and that the social variables that affect the giving of one generally have the same effect on the giving of the other, with two notable exceptions. Because the range in the amount of time different

56

people can give is considerably more limited than the range in the amount of money, not nearly as large a disproportion of volunteering comes from upper incomes as does the giving of money. Thus while 21 per cent of money contributions was projected to come from those with incomes of $50,000 or more, only five per cent of time given comes from the same segment of the population. Another significant difference between the giving of money and time that the survey finds is that instead of rising throughout life with the age of the giver, as the giving of money does on the average, the average of volunteer hours given peaks in the 35- to 44-year-old range and falls off markedly after that.

Where does the giving go? Most of all to religious institutions, but with an important qualification. The Interfaith Research Committee of the Commission conducted an extensive study of religious giving, drawing on unprecedented financial openness by the country's major denominations. This study indicates that religious giving (of money) may be substantially larger than generally estimated, but it also finds that more than one fifth of this giving goes ultimately to nonsacramental purposes. The two charts on the following page are based on these findings. One chart indicates amounts of giving in which both sacramental and nonsacramental uses of giving to religious groups are included in the figure for religious giving, the other in which the nonsacramental destinations of religious giving are assigned to other recipient categories.

Not only does giving come in different proportions from different income groups and go unequally to different areas of society, but if donees and donors are looked at together, it is evident that certain income levels of donor tend to prefer certain kinds of donee. Most noticeably, higher-income givers give in particular to educational and cultural organizations and hospitals while lower-income donors give above all to religion. The shares that three major philanthropic categories receive from each income group's overall giving are indicated in the chart on page 59.

Another cross-section of donor-donee giving patterns that was computed for the Commission looks at the average amount of yearly giving that each recipient category receives from indi-

WHERE THE GIVING GOES

Distribution of Private Philanthropy by Recipient, 1972
(In billions of dollars)

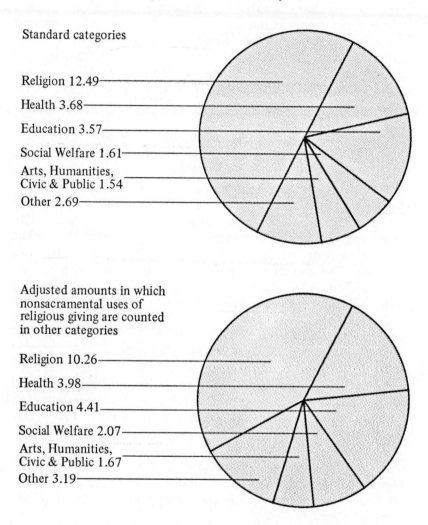

Standard categories

Religion 12.49

Health 3.68

Education 3.57

Social Welfare 1.61

Arts, Humanities,
Civic & Public 1.54

Other 2.69

Adjusted amounts in which
nonsacramental uses of
religious giving are counted
in other categories

Religion 10.26

Health 3.98

Education 4.41

Social Welfare 2.07

Arts, Humanities,
Civic & Public 1.67

Other 3.19

Sources: Interfaith Research Committee of Commission
on Private Philanthropy and Public Needs; and American
Association of Fund-Raising Counsel

58

WHO GIVES WHAT TO WHOM

Distribution of Giving to Major Donee Areas, by Income, 1972

Per cent of Total Giving of Each Income Group Going to:

▨ Religion   ☐ Federated Drives*   ▨ Special Areas**

Adjusted Gross Income	Religion	Federated Drives*	Special Areas**
Under $10,000	70%	13%	17%
$10,000 to $20,000	66%	15%	19%
$20,000 to $50,000	51%	17%	33%
$50,000 to $200,000	27%	17%	57%
$200,000 and over	7%	9%	84%

* Includes United Funds, Community Chests, etc.

** Includes educational institutions, museums, hospitals

Source: Commission on Private Philanthropy and Public Needs

59

viduals in each income group. These averages, shown on the table opposite, are based on 1970 income and giving amounts, and while many of these amounts probably have increased along with the overall rise in undeflated dollar amounts of giving since 1970, the wide ratios between giving averages presumably remain approximately the same.

Other Giving

The patterns of giving by other sources of philanthropy differ markedly from giving by living individuals as a whole, with religion the least favored by other sources instead of the most, and education one of the most favored donee areas instead of one of the least:

Charitable bequests, especially those from the highest-income benefactors, tend to reflect this inverse pattern to a considerable degree. Ten out of fourteen of the largest bequests in 1974 went to higher education.

Foundation grants from 1961 to 1973 have gone primarily to education (32 per cent of all major grants), followed by health (15 per cent), international activities (14 per cent), welfare (13 per cent), sciences (13 per cent), humanities (9 per cent, including the arts) and religion (4 per cent).

Corporate giving, according to a 1974 survey by The Conference Board and the Council for Financial Aid to Education, goes primarily to health and welfare organizations (38 per cent of corporate giving, most of it through federated drives such as United Way) and to education (35 per cent, nearly all of it for higher education), with civic (10 per cent) and cultural (7 per cent) causes representing other major recipient areas. Religion accounts for only one third of one per cent of corporate giving.

Changing Motivations

Such are the basic facts and figures on giving in the United States today. Beneath them lie an array of social and psycho-

Average Yearly Individual Giving to Major Donee Areas by Income Levels, 1970

Adjusted Gross Income	Reli-gion	Educa-tion	Hospi-tals	Health & Welfare	All Other*
$5,000 and below	$63	$1	$0	$10	$15
5,000 – 10,000	138	3	1	28	32
10,000 – 15,000	191	5	2	43	43
15,000 – 20,000	235	14	6	63	71
20,000 – 50,000	349	48	25	114	152
50,000 – 100,000	638	267	119	352	644
100,000 – 500,000	1,322	1,791	615	1,203	4,251
500,000 – 1,000,000	4,466	14,909	5,546	8,067	39,037
More than 1,000,000	7,073	45,866	14,688	14,430	175,219
Average Giving for All Incomes	$140	$9	$4	$34	$46

*Including giving to arts and cultural institutions and to private foundations

Source: Commission on Private Philanthropy and Public Needs

logical and historical patterns that in many respects are as complex as American society itself, and as full of changes and ambivalences.

Personal sacrifice for the community good has probably always been esteemed—and, in some eyes, suspect—and underlying motivations have perhaps always been complicated. But patterns of giving and the complex of motivations for giving have changed considerably over time, and unquestionably are continuing to change today. In mankind's early history, benevolence ended at the boundaries of the tribe or family. Within these boundaries, giving was hardly charitable in a modern sense because those who were able were expected, indeed required, to take care of the unable. There was none of the aspect of individual volition that is associated with modern giving. (Some social scientists feel that there is not as much of it now as we might pretend, that social pressures and fund-raising strategies literally leave little choice up to the individual giver. The Commission's sample survey of givers lends some support to this thesis: 30 per cent of higher-income contributors said they feel they are pressured into giving more time or money than they really want to.) As for strangers outside the tribe or family, only recently in the social evolution of humanity have outsiders been considered possible objects of concern, let alone sympathy and aid.

"The growth of civilization may be judged," F. Emerson Andrews, a leading analyst of philanthropy, has written, "by the extent to which the obligations of philanthropy have spread to include those whose fate was previously a matter of indifference—the slave, the poor, the barbarian, the enemy." Still, in the western world this expansion did not swiftly move the spirit of giving beyond what today might be called enlightened self-interest. In the Middle Ages, the wealthy were expected to make gifts and bequests to the church, not so much for the sake of the church or the "pious causes" furthered by the gifts as for the giver's own redemption—"salvation at a price," as scholars have uneuphemistically termed it.

Not until the seventeenth century did the giver's salvation begin to count for less than the expected good to ultimate beneficiaries. Again, this was by no means a rapid shift, nor

62

has it been a complete one, even to this day. At the end of the seventeenth and beginning of the eighteenth century, one of America's most eloquent champions of philanthropy, Cotton Mather, articulated an exceedingly broad philosophy of giving and one that covers the wide spectrum of motivations that have been and often still are attributed to giving. As historian Robert Bremner writes in his survey of American philanthropy, "Mather regarded the performance of good works as an obligation owed to God rather than a means of salvation; yet he had no doubt that God would punish the unfaithful steward. Moreover, doing good was a reward in itself. To help the unfortunate was an honor, a privilege, 'an incomparable pleasure.' Mather cited an entire catalogue of worldly advantages including long life and business success he thought would surely accrue to the benevolent. Besides, as Mather took pains to point out, doing good was sound social policy, a mild but effective instrument of social control. Pious example, moral leadership, voluntary effort and private charity were the means by which competing and conflicting interests in society might be brought into harmony."

The Institutionalization of Philanthropy

For much of recorded history, the church served as the main motivator and institutional channel of philanthropy, and this was so as much in early America as in medieval Europe. Church groups in the new settlements of the New World served as the principal recipients of alms and as dispensers, to the worthy, of goods, services and advice. With four out of ten philanthropic dollars still going to, or through, religious groups, religion continues to play a major role in both the motivations and dispensations of philanthropy. The course of modern giving, however, can be seen largely as a process of secularization and of institutionalization outside of organized religion.

A major shift in the spirit of American philanthropy was marked and to a considerable extent influenced by an article entitled "Wealth," published in the North American Review in

June, 1889. The author was Andrew Carnegie, steel manufacturer and philanthropist, and his message was manifold. The wealthy, he said, should administer their wealth as a public trust during their lifetimes because, having proved themselves in the struggle for commercial success, they were particularly fitting agents of the public trust. "Administrators of surplus wealth" was his term for philanthropists and his "gospel of wealth" focused not on the poor so much as the ambitious. He wrote of "ladders upon which the aspiring can rise," and directed his money toward the building of libraries, parks, concert halls, museums and educational institutions with a practical slant.

Carnegie and a contemporary fellow "millionaire," John D. Rockefeller, both felt that wealth carried obligations to society, yet both had so much of it that they had trouble giving it away as fast as they and their enterprises earned it. Both made vast fortunes in business, so perhaps it was inevitable that they eventually set up businesslike structures for giving. "If a combination to do business is effective in saving wastes and getting better results," asked Rockefeller, "why is not combination far more important in philanthropic work? Let us erect a foundation, a trust, and engage directors who will make it a life work to manage, with our personal cooperation, this business of benevolence properly and effectively."

Thus, with the arrival of the twentieth century was born the first of the large, wide-ranging foundations as major institutions of philanthropic giving. Some 25,000 private grant-making foundations exist today with combined assets, it is estimated, of around $25 billion. The great majority have modest resources and highly specialized aims. But scores operate, with wide discretionary funding powers and multimillion-dollar annual budgets, as regular, often highly visible sources of private funds for public purposes. Most larger foundations have full-time professional staffs who are paid to provide sophisticated analysis and management to the "business of benevolence."

The institutionalization of philanthropy has proceeded by smaller steps through the tax laws as well—in the spread of property tax exemption and, in 1917, the enactment of the federal income tax deduction for charitable giving, developments that are discussed in Chapter V. Since the beginning of this century, the United States has also witnessed the development of professional fund raising, of techniques for collecting sizable sums in relatively small individual amounts. The spirit of giving was by no means limited to millionaires but became embedded in American ways as part of a growing self-image of Americans as a generous and altruistic people.

The Importance of Private Giving

Any survey of giving in the United States would be misleading if it suggested that philanthropy was simply and universally welcomed along its course as a matter of gratuitous generosity by the giver and unquestioned benefit to the recipient. In fact, private giving for public purposes has regularly throughout American history been the subject of both pragmatic and ideological skepticism, reflecting the social climates and attitudes of different times, particularly attitudes toward unequal wealth and the wealthy from which such a disproportionate amount of philanthropy flows.

Doubts about philanthropy, its equity and its accountability, have arisen with particular force in recent years, and these doubts and their implications are considered later in this report. Yet, if some aspects of philanthropy are reasonable grounds for concern in a democratic society, the implications of little or no philanthropy may be grounds for even greater concern in a pluralistic society. The case for private giving for public purposes—on at least as large a scale as exists today in the United States—comes to rest to a major degree on the desirability of there existing nongovernmental organizations operating for public purposes alongside government, and on the practical reality that such organizations cannot depend on government for support and still remain nongovernmental in any significant sense—certainly not, at least, if they are totally dependent on government. While this report considers the growing need—the desperate appeals in some cases—for governmental funds by many traditional parts of the nonprofit sector,

65

Commission studies of these areas stress the importance of a continuing input of private giving and volunteer help in order to maintain standards of excellence and preseve a degree of independence.

Speaking for one of the major traditional recipients of private giving, higher education, one study asserts that private institutions of higher education "must have these funds to ensure their autonomous survival." Like a number of other studies this one refers to flexibility provided by private funds and to "an important measure of stability to help offset sudden shifts in federal funding." The report refers to "the accumulated wisdom that institutions of higher education are best able to perform their functions when they are funded from more than one source, with more than a single taste." Finding an emphasis in public health programs on short-range and immediate problems, a report on the role of philanthropy in the health field emphasizes the need for private support for long-range purposes—the advancing of national medical care standards, for instance. "Private philanthropy will be the only source of support," the report states, "which will enable independent health institutions to pursue such alternative priorities." (The bulk of federal spending on health—79 cents of every health dollar—is for supporting existing health service activities, whereas 89 cents of every foundation dollar spent in the field goes for longer-term, "capital goods" projects and research, according to a study by the National Planning Association.)

The ability to carry out and respond to different priorities— which is at the very heart of the pluralistic value of voluntary organizations—is what private philanthropy ultimately affords, and even a relatively small amount of private funding can help provide a substantial degree of such diversity. In several instances, for example, Commission research took note of the increasing flow of private funds to public institutions of higher education and it was asserted that even in such governmentally controlled institutions private funds can provide an "edge of quality," through special programs and expenditures above and beyond what governmental appropriations can or usually do allow. In a Commission report on philanthropy in the city of Des Moines the mayor of that city found the flexibility of

66

private funding, although relatively small in dollar amounts compared to the city budget, to be an absolutely essential complement to public funding in providing for basic municipal needs. "Without private funding," he said, "the public services and improvement practices would collapse." A study of philanthropy in England, where voluntary organizations are generally much more dependent on government financing than in the United States, similarly finds for that country's voluntary sector an important role for even a small degree of private funding alongside public support. Because of private funds the people who run such organizations, notes the study, "are less likely to become (or feel that they are becoming) simple agents for carrying out plans developed in [government offices]."

Some kinds of voluntary organizations can hardly be expected to function at all, or must function in fundamentally different ways, unless their basic support is private giving. A 1973 study on environmental groups found, for instance, that those that relied on membership support tended to be more involved in public advocacy on environmental issues and to use more militant tactics than did groups that depended on government grants (or on corporate and foundation grants, for that matter). Many new "public-interest" and "grass-roots" groups in areas such as environmentalism, consumerism and legal activism exist at least in part, and in some cases very large part, to actively criticize and challenge government, and they must rely entirely on nongovernmental support to be effective in this adversary role.

Philanthropy and the Powerless

Private giving today also plays a role which government by its own institutional nature is unable to play and which, indeed, much of philanthropy itself is hesitant to venture into. As described in a Commission report on philanthropy in the San Francisco area, this role is to help "submerged people who are trying to get ahead." The role may also be defined as helping to empower the powerless of American society, often nonwhite, non-middleclass groups that through their own resources have been able to exercise little influence on the priorities and processess of majoritarian government or of other institutional areas of our society. Giving for this purpose differs from old-style charity, from the filling of basic needs of the poor and underprivileged. As consciously seen by some of the donors and donees, such giving is more a matter of helping groups to organize and act so as to be able to effectively exact social and economic and political benefits or "rights" from society and its institutions.

A Commission study on philanthropy and the powerless provides a number of examples of such giving—and getting—in recent years, among them:

—*The welfare rights movement.* Led by the National Welfare Rights Organization, which was founded in 1967, this movement helped dramatize and bring to the nation's attention and the attention of government leaders the plight of welfare recipients. It also served, through the emergence of many local groups, to instruct welfare recipients in their legal rights regarding procedures and levels of assistance and to inform many non-recipients of their eligibility for aid. The major support of NWRO and an associated foundation came from church groups and a number of the more "activist" foundations.

—*Growth of minority business enterprises.* Foundations, churches and corporations have contributed substantial sums in recent years to help minority group members start or sustain businesses, mainly in urban areas. Because of this help, many medium-sized firms owned by minority group members have been launched, and a sizable portion have succeeded and have grown.

—*American Indians' rights.* In the past few years church groups and foundations have devoted an increasing amount of funds to Indian programs; because of the federal government's extensive involvement in Indian affairs, much of this giving has gone to political lobbying and to legal activism through organizations such as the Native American Legal Defense and Education Fund. Defining and extending the power of Indian tribal governments and tribal legal institutions has been among the efforts funded for the purpose of empowering what in many regards has been the most powerless segment in American society.

—Institutional reform. In the past decade philanthropy has supported efforts to reform major institutions and to help establish rights and procedures to protect the interests of members or inmates of such institutions. Prison reform efforts, for example, have resulted in the elimination of some of the more blatant brutalities of prison life and in introducing an element of due process in the handling of prisoners. Funds that have gone to advocates of military justice have been successful in halting the widespread practice of issuing less than honorable discharges, which did not entail as stringent legal procedures as did dishonorable discharges but which often had the same effect: they could wreck a veteran's career or severely restrict his job opportunities. While most philanthropy for institutional reform has involved public institutions, a notable success in this area was centered on a private one, the United Mine Workers' union. Foundation support was instrumental in the successful effort to rid the union of a deeply entrenched and corrupt leadership and introduce a reform-minded administration in its place.

As the Commission's report on philanthropy and the powerless notes, giving for all such purposes amounts to a small percentage of overall giving, a grossly inadequate amount, in some eyes, in light of the needs and the challenges involved. By one estimate, less than one per cent of foundation giving in 1972, 1973 and 1974 went specifically for the benefit of social and ethnic minorities. And in a paper for the Commission entitled, "Who's Funding the Women's Movement?," the answer given is that very few institutional philanthropic sources are. A survey of feminist organizations found that only around twenty foundations and a dozen corporations were funding such groups and those that were doing so were doing it at low levels. In 1972 through 1974, it is estimated, less than one fifth of one per cent of foundations' grants went to "projects designed to improve the status of women." The conclusion of the paper is that "the women's movement has been almost entirely shut out by the philanthropic establishment."*

At the same time, some feminist organizations have had

*See comment by FRANCES T. FARENTHOLD, GRACIELA OLIVAREZ AND ALTHEA T. L. SIMMONS, page 197.

better success in raising money by direct mail solicitation. So while the amounts of money going to such causes may be seen as inadequate—or, in some eyes, as excessive because of the social friction involved—the changes being sought almost surely would be slower in coming, if ever, were it not for the practice of private voluntary giving.

NOT KEEPING PACE

In light of the continuing, vital role of private giving for public purposes in American society, one major fact about philanthropy that stands out in the Commission studies should be a matter of considerable concern to Americans. It is to the Commission. This is the evidence that while private giving is still large in the United States by comparison with other countries, and while it has grown continuously in current dollar measurements ever since estimates of philanthropy have been compiled, it has not kept pace with the growth of the economy over the last decade, and in constant, uninflated dollars, it has fallen off absolutely in the last few years.

As noted earlier, measuring philanthropic giving is a complex and imperfect art. While the federal government keeps tabs on itemized deductions for giving, two out of every three taxpayers use the standard deduction and therefore include no specific account of charitable giving in their tax returns. Various means of estimating undeclared giving have developed in recent years, however, and even by the most optimistic estimates, those put together annually by the American Association of Fund-Raising Counsel, total giving has declined almost steadily as a per cent of gross national product since 1969—from 1.98 per cent then to 1.80 per cent in 1974.

Ralph L. Nelson, an economist at Queens College, who has made several independent studies of philanthropic giving for the National Bureau of Economic Research, the Carnegie Corporation and the United States Census Bureau, comes to even less promising conclusions in a study for the Commission. Among his findings: "The evidence seems to point quite consistently to the conclusion that, in the twelve-year period from 1960 to 1972, private philanthropy's share of the American economy experienced considerable shrinkage."

Nelson's studies indicate that giving by individuals, in particular, the cornerstone of private support for nonprofit organizations, has failed to keep up with gross national product or personal income for a number of years. As a proportion of personal income, Nelson calculates, giving by individuals has dropped by about 15 per cent between 1960 and 1972, from 1.97 per cent of personal income in 1960 to 1.67 per cent in 1972.

A refinement on this barometer that might be said to better measure the degree of personal sacrifice in giving is tabulated by the Treasury Department's Office of Tax Analysis. In a table that looks at tax itemizers' "net contributions"—which are defined as contributions minus the reduction in federal income tax that donors receive because of the tax deduction for these contributions—giving is seen as dropping from 3.47 per cent of adjusted gross income in 1956 to 2.10 per cent in 1970.

Reasons for the Decline

Why has there been at least a relative falloff in giving—by virtually every reckoning? The ravages of inflation and recession no doubt account for a good deal of the recent decline. In the Commission's survey of giving, the most frequent explanation by those who gave little or nothing to philanthropic causes was, not surprisingly, that they did not feel they could afford to give. Yet the problems of the economy do nothing to explain the sluggishness, at best, of giving in the boom years of the sixties and early seventies.

Declines in the largest category of donations—to religious institutions—account for a sizable portion of the decline in overall giving. Religious contributions dropped from 49.4 per cent of all giving in 1964 to 43.1 per cent in 1974 according to the American Association of Fund-Raising Counsel, a falloff that is quite expectable in light of the fact that church attendance has declined about nine per cent since 1958 and enrollments in parochial schools, which have traditionally received about 15 per cent of religious giving, have dropped off by one third from their high point in 1964-65.

As noted earlier, low- and middle-income contributors provide the bulk of donations, and it is significant that in terms of net contributions—or out-of-pocket costs once tax savings are calculated—it is in the $10,000 to $25,000 income range that giving has fallen the most in recent years. This is not necessarily because those whose incomes have stayed within that range are giving less; the decrease may reflect the generally rapid increase in average incomes in the period studied (1956 to 1970) and the possibility that many of the large number of taxpayers who newly arrived in the $10,000 to $25,000 income range may have lagged in expanding their giving from what they were accustomed to contributing at lower income levels.

Tax inducements to giving are examined later in this report. Increases in the level of the standard deduction in recent years may have had some depressing effect on giving. In theory, at least, they should have lessened the impulse to give, because charitable contributions are not deductible if the standard deduction is claimed in place of itemized deductions.

Are other, perhaps profounder factors at work as well in diminishing the level of giving? Although it is not easily tested, one distinct possibility is that because the scope of government has expanded and continues to expand into areas that are principally identified in the public eye with philanthropy, Americans may be less inclined to feel that giving for public purposes is important. They may feel that government is already taking care of much of what they are asked to contribute to, or that it should. In interviews for a series of Commission reports on philanthropy in five American cities, a United Way fund raiser in the San Francisco area cited such an attitude as the reason for resistance to giving by one professional group. "A lot of doctors," she said, "still tell us, 'I thought the government was doing all that sort of thing now. What are my taxes going for?' "

At the same time, other evidence suggests that while the level of giving has declined, the spirit of giving may not be waning so much as changing its objects and objectives, as it has done in the past. A Gallup poll in 1972 found that 71 per cent of Americans said that they thought private giving was as important as ever or more so. And successes in regularly raising

72

large sums of money by many new and some not so new organizations—from United Ways to Common Cause to the National Rifle Association—indicate a willingness by Americans to privately, voluntarily support nonprofit causes that they believe in and that they feel depend on private support.

Indeed, in terms of volunteer time given, as contrasted to financial support, there has been an impressive increase in recent years on both relative and absolute scales. According to a 1974 Census Bureau survey commissioned by the government's agency for voluntary service, ACTION, nearly one out of every four Americans (24 per cent) over the age of 13 does some form of volunteer work as compared to less than one out of five in 1965—the finding of a Labor Department survey that year. Not only are more Americans contributing time and labor, but they are contributing more of it. In 1974, 63 per cent of those who said they did volunteer work estimated that they did more than 25 hours of such work a year. In 1965, only 54 per cent said they did as much volunteer work.

Financial support, for that matter, has held its own in most nonreligious areas, at least until the last few years of national economic disarray; as previously noted, much of the overall decline in giving is accounted for by a dropoff in religious contributions. Two relatively new categories of secular giving in the compilation by the American Association of Fund-Raising Counsel—Arts and Humanities and Civic and Public giving—have grown faster than the economy. In the process, they have been claiming an ever larger share of the philanthropic dollar over the last decade.

Giving, in other words, has hardly remained static in either its destinations or motivations. The graph on page 74 shows the relative shifts among broad categories of recipients over the past third of a century. Giving has shifted even more than indicated because the graph does not show shifts within categories, which in such vast and amorphous areas as social welfare and health have been very sizable. However, the fluidity of giving patterns is still evident.

Whether recent trends will continue in the same direction or themselves will shift, as they have done in the past, or will be joined by major new kinds of recipients remains to be seen,

CHANGES IN GIVING

Percentage of Total Giving
Going to Each Recipient Area, 1940-1974

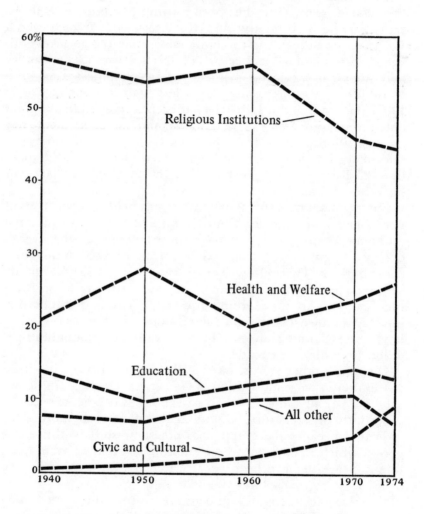

Source: Commission on Private Philanthropy and Public Needs

74

and in part to be guided by government tax policy, which as this report later examines can influence both the amount and direction of contributions. But the likelihood that changes are in the making is the one constant about philanthropy that can probably be counted upon, especially in a day when very little on the social landscape appears to be standing still for very long. Some of these shifts are likely to be painful to nonprofit areas that depend on recent or, in some cases, long-established patterns of philanthropic giving, but the very prospect of change can and should be regarded as one of the strengths and vitalities of private giving—the fact that giving is fluid and adjustable enough to reflect the inevitably shifting patterns and priorities of any society that is itself strong and vital and responsive to the free choices and inclinations of its members.

Sources for Chapter II

ACTION, *American Volunteers 1974*, U.S. Government Printing Office, 1975.

American Association of Fund-Raising Counsel, Inc., *Giving U.S.A., 1975 Annual Report.*

Thomas R. Asher, *Public Needs, Public Policy and Philanthropy.**

Robert J. Blendon, *The Changing Role of Private Philanthropy in Health Affairs.**

Landrum R. Bolling, *Statement Submitted to Subcommittee on Foundations of Senate Finance Committee*, June 1974.

Daniel P. Bourque and Rory Redondo, The National Planning Association, *A Comparison of Federal Government Expenditures and Private Foundation Grants for Health and Health-Related Activities for Fiscal Year 1973.**

Blair T. Bower, *The Role of Private Philanthropy in Relation to Environment— Pollution.**

Gerard M. Brannon and James Strnad, *Alternative Approaches to Encouraging Philanthropic Activities.**

George F. Break, *Charitable Contributions under the Federal Individual Income Tax: Some Alternative Policy Options.**

Robert H. Bremner, *Private Philanthropy and Public Needs: An Historical Perspective.**

Sarah C. Carey, *Philanthropy and the Powerless.**

John J. Carson and Harry V. Hodson, eds., *Philanthropy in the '70's: An Anglo-American Discussion*, Council on Foundations Inc., New York, 1973.

Earl F. Cheit and Theodore E. Lobman III, *Private Philanthropy and Higher Education.**

Wilbur J. Cohen, *Some Aspects of Evolving Social Policy in Relation to Private Philanthropy.**

Commission on Foundations and Private Philanthropy, *Foundations, Private Giving and Public Policy*, University of Chicago Press, Chicago, 1970.

Committee on the Law and Practice Relating to Charitable Trusts (Nathan Committee), *Report on Charitable Trusts,* Her Majesty's Stationery Office, London, 1952.

The Conference Board and the Council for Financial Aid to Education, *Annual Survey of Corporation Contributions 1974.*

Council on Foundations, Inc., *Private Foundations and the 1969 Tax Reform Act.**

Fred R. Crawford, *Non-Economic Motivational Factors in Philanthropic Behavior.**

Frank G. Dickinson, *The Changing Position of Philanthropy in the American Economy*, National Bureau of Economic Research, New York, 1970.

Solomon Fabricant, "Philanthropy in the American Economy," *Foundation News*, September-October, 1969, Vol. X, No. 5.

Martin S. Feldstein, *Tax Incentives and Charitable Contributions in the United States: A Microeconometric Analysis.**

Martin S. Feldstein and Amy Taylor, *The Income Tax and Charitable Contributions: Estimates and Simulations with the Treasury Tax Files.**

Caryl P. Haskins, *The Role of Private Philanthropy and Public Support of Science in the United States.**

Caroline Hightower, *A Report on the Arts.**

Interfaith Research Committee of the Commission on Private Philanthropy and Public Needs, Stuart M. Lewis, Project Coordinator, *Study of Religious Receipts and Expenditures in the United States.**

Hans H. Jenny, *Philanthropy in Higher Education.**

C. Harry Kahn, *Personal Deductions in the Federal Income Tax*, Princeton University Press, 1960.

Calvin Kentfield, *Private Philanthropy in Des Moines.**

Reynold Levy and Waldemar A. Nielsen, *An Agenda for the Future.**

Paul R. McDaniel, *Study of Federal Matching Grants for Charitable Contributions.**

William G. McLoughlin, "Changing Patterns of Protestant Philanthropy 1607-1969," in *The Religious Situation*, Beacon Press, Boston, 1969.

James N. Morgan, Richard F. Dye and Judith Hybels, *Results from Two National Surveys of Philanthropic Activity.**

National Center for Voluntary Action, *A Report on Voluntary Activities and Leadership Opinion.**

Ralph L. Nelson, *Private Giving in the American Economy, 1960-1972.**

Ralph L. Nelson, *Estimates of Private Giving for 1973 and 1974.**

Ralph L. Nelson, *Analysis of Trends in Giving Since 1960.**

David Owen, *English Philanthropy, 1660-1960*, Harvard University Press, Cambridge, 1964.

John P. Persons, John J. Osborn Jr. and Charles F. Feldman, *Criteria for Exemption Under Section 501(c)(3).**

Jack Shepherd, *Passing the Buck: Philanthropy in San Francisco.**

David Horton Smith and Burt R. Baldwin, "Voluntary Association and Volunteering in the United States," in *Voluntary Action Research 1974*, D.C. Heath & Company, Boston, 1975.

Lawrence M. Stone, *The Charitable Foundation: Its Governance.**

Emil M. Sunley Jr., *Dimensions of Charitable Giving Reported on Federal Estate, Gift, and Fiduciary Tax Returns.**

Mary Jean Tully, *Who's Funding the Women's Movement?**

United States Senate, Report of Proceedings, Subcommittee on Foundations, Committee on Finance, *Impact of Current Economic Crisis on Funds and Recipients of Foundation Money*, November 25, 1974.

Thomas Vasquez, *Corporate Giving Measurements.**

Joseph L. Vigilante and Ruth Kantrow, *The Voluntary Social Agency Experiments, Innovates, Demonstrates, and Influences Public Social Policy: The Community Service Society of New York 1930-1970.**

Richard E. Wagner, *Death, Taxes, and Charitable Bequests: A Survey of Issues and Options.**

Laurens Williams and Donald V. Moorehead, *An Analysis of the Federal Tax Distinctions Between Public and Private Charitable Organizations.**

Ellen Winston, *Some Aspects of Private Philanthropy in Relation to Social Welfare.**

Paul N. Ylvisaker and Jane H. Mavity, *The Role of Private Philanthropy in Public Affairs.**

*Denotes reports and studies undertaken for the Commission.

III

THE HARD ECONOMICS
OF NONPROFIT ACTIVITY

In the midst of an economic downturn more severe than any since the Great Depression, two headlined news stories were among those that seemed to epitomize the economy's disarray. In the spring of 1975, the Ford Foundation announced that it was cutting its staff and its disbursements by half following the fall in value of the foundation's assets by one third. A few months earlier, Harvard University was reported to be "bracing for hard times." Layoffs for the Ford Foundation and hard times for Harvard University? The nation's largest foundation, with assets of two billion dollars—down from three billion—and our most abundantly endowed university—holding more than a billion dollars worth of assets—probably symbolize in many eyes the very essence of institutional financial solidity, even opulence. And if they were in trouble . . .

But if these particular bits of economic bad news may have surprised many readers or only affirmed their gloomiest apprehensions about the course of the economy, the difficulties of the Ford Foundation and Harvard University hardly represented a sudden and novel development in the common terrain of the two large institutions, the nonprofit sector. The sector has been in financial trouble for years. Pushes and pulls of economy-wide inflation and recession have certainly intensified the sector's problems. Plunging stock prices eroded endowments, such as the Ford Foundation's, and recession has inhibited private giving. Meanwhile inflation has sent expenditures soaring, putting even greater strains on depleted revenue bases. Among the many tolls of inflation: fuel bills at some universities and colleges have tripled within a matter of a few years.

Laments about economic and financial difficulties have, of course, been heard throughout the economy in recent years; the voluntary sector has hardly been alone in suffering the strains of inflation and recession. Still, indications are that the economic maladies of the nonprofit sector not only reflect economy-wide strains but are also the result of dynamics endemic to the nonprofit sector in particular. In fact, the financial difficulties of many parts of the nonprofit sector were a matter of growing concern even in the midst of general prosperity. In the late 1960's, for instance, when the economy was booming, one survey of the philanthropic landscape found matters bad and probably getting worse. "Even as things stand right now," said this report, "many philanthropic institutions are already living with an acute financial crisis, and if things go on as they are without remedy, the crisis will become all the more acute in the future." That things were expected to go on as they were was indicated in a concluding passage of the report: ". . . Without important new sources of funds amounting to many billions of dollars, our society will feel the full force of what can be called the charitable crisis of the 1970's."

Financial Crisis

Now, in the mid-70's, acute crisis does indeed appear to describe the state of many parts of the nonprofit sector; existence of whole areas within the sector may be threatened. Headlines regularly document this dire prospect, and it is the common theme of the reports this Commission has received from experts in the many different areas of the nonprofit sector. "During the last several years," writes Hans H. Jenny, vice president of Wooster College, "beginning some time in the late 1960's, higher education finance has suffered a gradual deterioration in both public and private sectors." The severest deterioration of all among institutions of higher learning has been suffered by the private liberal arts college, so much so that, according to one Commission report, "to talk of the liberal arts college's disappearance . . . is not to indulge in idle speculation." Indeed, around 150 private colleges have already disappeared, shut down, since 1969. Another area of nonpublic education, private pre-college schooling, may be in even worse shape financially. "In the long run," says a report on this area, "if the economic trends continue, the vast majority of nonpublic schools seem doomed, the exceptions being schools enjoying the support of the well-to-do or heavy subsidies from a few remaining religious groups with conservative theologies or strong ethnic emphasis." In fact, although the situation may have stabilized in their regard of late, parochial schools, which account for the large majority of private primary and secondary institutions, have already been closing their doors by the hundreds around the country in recent years.

Nonprofit arts organizations have similarly been in financial trouble for a number of years on nearly every front, from symphony orchestras to museums. Social service organizations have been slashing their budgets and reducing their staffs in order to stay afloat, or in a number of cases have gone out of business completely.

Not all nonprofit groups, of course, are suffering financial problems, and indeed a broad area of smallscale nonprofit organizations on the frontier of nonprofit activity have relatively minute budgets and modest fixed costs and, if they have problems, they tend to think of them more as political than economic (see Chapter VII). Still, much of the traditional, highly institutionalized part of the nonprofit sector is in trouble, in many cases, profound trouble.

The sluggishness of private giving, examined in the previous chapter, is clearly a factor in the economic plight of many nonprofit organizations. Erratic government funding has also accounted for financial strains in some areas of the nonprofit sector. Colleges and universities have built up facilities and staffs in response to government programs, for instance, only to find funding for some programs drastically reduced within a few years of their initiation. But the revenue side of the sector's financial ledgers tells only part of the story. The other part is about extraordinary increases in expenses, many of which appear to be beyond the control or limitation of nonprofit causes, some of which seem to be part of the special economics of nonprofit activity.

RISING COSTS

A major factor in rising expenses is the fact that the costs of goods and services used in nonprofit activities have been going up significantly more rapidly than in the economy as a whole, for a number of years. Nonprofit health institutions, for instance, have had to contend with the harsh fact of economic life that since 1960 medical care costs have risen half again as fast as consumer prices in general. Higher education costs similarly rose about 76 per cent between 1963-64 and 1973-74, compared to 49 per cent for the economy-wide cost-of-living index.

An overall estimate of the rate of increased costs of all charitable nonprofit services has been made by economist Ralph Nelson, who has calculated price rises in various special areas of the nonprofit sector. From 1960 to 1972, he figures, or before double-digit inflation set in for the economy as a whole, the annual growth rate in prices for the nonprofit sector was more than 4 per cent compared to 3 per cent for the whole economy.

Some measure of how this rise in prices has eroded the purchasing power of nonprofit revenues is given in special price-deflating calculations by Nelson. The standard way of looking at the trends in philanthropic funds from year to year has been to deflate money figures by the same proportions that the consumer price index or the gross national product is discounted in order to abstract out price rises that do not reflect "real" economic changes. Yet such mathematical adjustments fail to reckon with the fact that costs in nonprofit activity have risen significantly faster than in the economy as a whole. In order to take account of these steeper price rises, Nelson deflates private giving according to different price patterns in different nonprofit areas. His conclusion: instead of doubling, as private giving has done in inflated dollars, or rising by more than half, which is the picture that emerges when the usual, economy-wide deflation factor is applied to philanthropy, total private giving increased the purchasing power of philanthropic organizations by a very modest 28 per cent between 1960 and 1972, from $9.3 billion to $11.9 billion. By comparison, in the same

82

period of rapid economic growth, gross national product increased more than twice as much as private philanthropic funds in real purchasing power—by 62 per cent.

The Cost of Being "Labor Intensive"

Why has there been a sizable, and from the standpoint of many nonprofit institutions, debilitating difference in price changes between the nonprofit sector and the economy as a whole? The most frequent explanation is that much nonprofit activity is comparatively "labor intensive": because it is involved mainly in the provision of services rather than the manufacture of products, the nonprofit sector's primary resource is human labor. In higher education, for instance, up to 85 per cent of the budget goes to salaries and wages. Arts organizations typically devote well over half of their budgets to personnel costs. For the theatre, the ratio is 62 per cent; opera, 66 per cent; symphony orchestras, 77 per cent; ballet, 62 per cent. The high proportion of labor usage by nonprofit services has meant more steeply rising prices partly because labor costs in general have risen faster than other prices in recent decades. Moreover, while many· industries have been able to dampen the impact of higher labor costs by introducing labor-saving technology, the nature of much nonprofit activity is such that it does not lend itself to such economizings. A 1974 Ford Foundation study on the performing arts explains the strains this limitation builds into the economics of philanthropy. "The level of costs is set by the general economy," says that study, "which is based on an industrial technology that enables output per manhour to increase steadily. But the technology of live performance has no equivalent capacity to increase productivity. A play or a symphony written two hundred years ago still has to be handcrafted by the same number of performers working the same length of time as they did at its premiere." Much the same can be said for seminars or medical examinations, sociological research or family relations consultations, can be said, in effect, of much of the large array of services that nonprofit organizations provide.

Not only is the nonprofit sector less able to save on labor costs, but the wages and salaries it has to pay probably have risen faster than other wages and salaries in the economy. This is so in part because they have risen from a lower base: work for nonprofit organizations has traditionally been paid less than comparable work in business or government. But because of unionization, an increased minimum wage, and other factors, the gap between the third sector's wage and salary rates and those of the other two sectors has narrowed.

The Costs of Complexity

More difficult to put a quantitative yardstick to, but perhaps just as important in boosting the costs of certain areas of the nonprofit sector is the increasing complexity of many of the social and scientific problems and solutions that today concern nonprofit groups. Dr. John H. Knowles, president of the Rockefeller Foundation, emphasized this factor in testimony before the Senate Finance Committee, in the course of talking about the economic problems of nonprofit institutions. He spoke of "the complexities of a given social problem today . . . the complexities that face service organizations in education, health, transportation, day care, welfare reform, the plight of minority groups, you name it. Now in contrast to perhaps twenty or thirty years ago when one individual might be able to encompass this, researching the problems and trying to give us sufficient information to solve problems, today the problems are of such complexity that they require larger teams of interdisciplinarians or interdisciplinary work to resolve in a rational fashion the complex issues that face us. Twenty or thirty years ago we could support research on the development of the yellow fever vaccine which might have involved a small group of people. Today we have to support that same number plus a goodly number of economists, political scientists, cultural anthropologists to help us determine how we can use that information here and around the world, recognizing that there are social, economic and cultural determinants to the use of knowledge that we gained today that are much more heavily in-

84

volved in the successful amelioration of human misery."

A Commission report on philanthropy in the health field similarly finds that in recent years there have been "developments in medical science which added tremendously to the cost of medical research, education, and care." The report explains: "The development of more complicated diagnostic and therapeutic procedures carried out by new types of medical specialists, assisted by substantial numbers of technicians, heavily increased the cost of doing medical care research. Special facilities, expensive equipment, lengthening training programs have become a necessity in modern medical research. Along with this, medical and health professional education improved and increased in duration and expense, as did the need for added investment in buildings, equipment, faculty, and student aid. In addition, hospitals and clinics greatly expanded the quality and scope of their services . . ."

Many nonprofit organizations, in other words, not only have been unable to economize by reducing labor costs but actually face the need for more resources to tackle the same problems, as those problems' complexities have become more apparent and the tools for dealing with them more sophisticated.

The More Successful, the Greater the Deficit

Another expensive aspect of the economics of nonprofit activities is that many of these activities do not readily lend themselves to economies of scale. And this is the basis of a costly irony: the more successful philanthropic "pioneering" has been in terms of reaching more people, the greater the operating deficit faced by philanthropic organizations, or in many cases whole philanthropic areas.

Underlying this irony is the fact that philanthropic services by their very nature and philosophy rarely pay for themselves. One of the principles central to much philanthropy is the idea of extending help or cultural enrichment to individuals regardless of their ability to pay for it. Therefore, while many philanthropically supported services have users' fees attached to them, in very few cases do these fees begin to cover the full cost of supplying the services. Tuitions cover two thirds of the costs of educating a student, at best. Earned income in the performing arts, most of it from ticket sales, covers one half to two thirds of costs, depending on the art form. Admissions to museums account for only one third of operating expenses. Nonprofit medical care is one of the few nonprofit services that, in recent years, and in limited circumstances, is paid for nearly in full by its users.

So the more users there are the more unreimbursed expenses are incurred. And because there are few economies of scale, there are few counterbalancing savings through lower per-user costs of operation. This aspect of the economics of nonprofit activity has been particularly significant in recent years—and has contributed heavily to the financial strains of the nonprofit sector—precisely because of the extraordinary "success" of pioneering in expanding the ranks of users of nonprofit services. Spurred by a rapidly growing population and even more rapidly growing gross national product, higher education enrollments doubled during the 1960's. The sixties were also the decade of the "culture boom," in which arts activities flourished and spread widely, in many cases because of deliberate "outreach" programs. Health care organizations and facilities multiplied, too. And with this expansion, nothing spread so fast and so hugely as the need for greater revenues to fill the broadening gap between user payments and operating expenses. While some of this demand has been abating as the population structure changes and becomes less youth-heavy, and as the economy as a whole has, at least temporarily, stopped growing, the expansion of nonprofit services continues to take its toll. In areas such as education, overcapacity may be beginning to outweigh the direct burdens of expansion itself, as some institutions find they have built new high-overhead classrooms and have fewer students to fill them. In these cases, a devastating double-barrelled economics is at work: the strained finances of accommodating what was a steep increase in the number of users are built into institutions in the form of increased plant and payrolls, while today there are actually fewer users to help pay the bills.

Finally, new philanthropic groups with new purposes have

sprouted or grown large in recent years to compete for what limited philanthropic resources there are—groups oriented toward urban and racial problems, environmental and consumer organizations, and other politically and legally activist groups—all with their own appeals for support.

All told, the prevailing financial pattern of the nonprofit sector has become one of uncommonly higher costs, more resources required for old problems and new solutions, more users needing greater aggregate subsidies for traditional services and new, less traditional groups adding their claim to the philanthropic pie. And it has been, in terms of private support, a barely growing pie all this time, not growing at all of late in terms of the real purchasing power of private contributions. This is the pattern that underlies the very real financial difficulties—"crisis" is no hyperbole here—of the philanthropic world. The question, which has been painfully faced by many organizations within the nonprofit sector, particularly the larger, more traditional ones, is whether there is any recourse but to turn increasingly to government to allay the crisis. And the question that should be faced by the American public is what the implications, the challenges and the hazards of this direction may be in terms of the people served by these organizations and in terms of the broad pluralistic value of these organizations to society as a whole.

Sources for Chapter III

Robert J. Blendon, *The Changing Role of Private Philanthropy in Health Affairs.**

John J. Carson and Harry V. Hodson, eds., *Philanthropy in the '70's: An Anglo-American Discussion*, Council on Foundations, Inc., New York, 1973.

Earl F. Cheit and Theodore E. Lobman III, *Philanthropy and Higher Education.**

Commission on Foundations and Private Philanthropy, *Foundations, Private Giving and Public Policy*, University of Chicago Press, Chicago, 1970.

Council on Foundations, Inc., *Private Foundations and the 1969 Tax Reform Act.**

Donald A. Erickson, *Philanthropy, Public Needs and Nonpublic Schools.**

Solomon Fabricant, "Philanthropy in the American Economy," *Foundation News*, September-October 1969, Vol. X, No. 5.

Caroline Hightower, *A Report on the Arts.**

Hans H. Jenny, *Philanthropy in Higher Education.**

Julian H. Levi, *Financing Education and the Effect of the Tax Laws.**

Reynold Levy and Waldemar A. Nielsen, *An Agenda for the Future.**

Richard W. Lyman, "In Defense of the Public Sector," *Daedalus*, Winter, 1975.

National Center for Voluntary Action, *A Report on Voluntary Activities and Leadership Opinion.**

Ralph L. Nelson, *Private Giving and the American Economy, 1960-1972.**

David Owen, *English Philanthropy, 1660-1960*, Harvard University Press, Cambridge, 1964.

United States Department of Health, Education and Welfare, *HEW News*, September 2, 1974.

United States Senate, Report of Proceedings, Subcommittee on Foundations, Committee on Finance, *Impact of Current Economic Crisis on Foundations and Recipients of Foundation Money*, November 25, 1974.

Ellen Winston, *Some Aspects of Private Philanthropy in Relation to Social Welfare.**

Adam Yarmolinsky, *The Tax Legislative Process and the Appropriations Process.**

*Denotes reports and studies undertaken for the Commission.

IV

THE STATE AS A
MAJOR "PHILANTHROPIST"

"Thus far, neither the shillings of the workingman nor the guineas from British business have markedly relieved the pressures on philanthropic agencies. Of infinitely greater consequence has been the emergence of the state itself as a major philanthropist and benefactor of the voluntary service."

This assessment of the course of British philanthropy, made in the mid-1960's in a seminal work on the subject by David Owen of Harvard University, applies in essence to American philanthropy in the mid-1970's. In recent years, government has emerged in the United States as a major "philanthropist," *the* major philanthropist in a number of the principal, traditional areas of philanthropy.

By most definitions, including the Commission's, the government does not and cannot literally play the role of philanthropist because part of the basic definition of philanthropy is its private, nongovernmental nature. Yet as a funder of nonprofit organizations and activities, government ranks, figuratively at least, as a very sizable "philanthropist" indeed. In 1974, according to the Commission's estimates (see p. 35), government funds accounted for about $23 billion of the revenues of nonprofit organizations compared to around $25 billion from all private sources of giving combined. At the same time, government has absorbed, and probably will continue to absorb, many philanthropic functions or services, either through the spread of public institutions and agencies that are counterparts of private organizations or through social programs that render certain philanthropic functions and services obsolete or redundant.

Government's expanding role as a "philanthropist" is roughly indexed by the growth rate of government non-defense spending as compared with private giving. In current dollars, such expenditures at all levels of government quadrupled from 1960 through 1974, while giving increased two and a half times in the same period. Government's non-defense spending has expanded in the process from nine times that of philanthropic giving to fourteen and a half times as much.

The growing role of government in philanthropy—or at least what have been considered philanthropic purposes—is evident at every turn in the nonprofit sector. In 1930, federal, state and local governments together spent about as much as private sources in the area of medical research and health facility construction. By 1973, government was spending three and a half times as much, and this in a health field where private philanthropy has maintained one of its strongest thrusts. In medical and health spending as a whole, the change has been even greater. In 1930, the federal government was spending only 15 per cent more than private philanthropy. In 1973, it was spending nearly seven times as much.

The dominance of government support and public institutions in higher education has been more gradual, but no less pronounced. For most of American history, private support has been by far the most important element in higher education. A study for the Commission by Earl F. Cheit, associate director of the Carnegie Council on Policy Studies in Higher Education, notes that a century ago all public funds accounted for only 10 per cent of higher education's income. Tuition accounted for 30 per cent, private giving, 60 per cent. But public spending passed private during World War II, and today the relative support of public and private funds are almost exactly the reverse of what they were a century ago, with tuition, interestingly enough, accounting for almost the same proportion today as it did then, midway between the two extremes.

The GI Bill, which established tuition and living-cost allowances for veterans who went to college, provided the major impetus to increased public spending in higher education after World War II. This student payment program could be used at private as well as public institutions, and it helped support both kinds of institutions. Meantime expanding enrollments, spurred by the GI Bill, by prosperity and by a growing college-age population, required new facilities. So public institutions were enlarged or in cases such as the New York State University, system were virtually started from scratch to meet the demand. Private higher education expanded as well; in fact, enrollments today in private colleges and universities are at an all-time high. But because of the limited supply of private funds, private higher education was unable to grow as fast as publicly funded institutions. Thus, from 1960 there has been a gradual decline in the proportion of private colleges and universities and a steeper falloff in the ratio of students attending private institutions. About two thirds of all institutions of higher learning were private in 1960. Today the proportion is nearer one half. In 1950, slightly over one half of all students were enrolled in private institutions. Today fewer than one quarter of college and university students go to private institutions.

From Private Beneficence to Public Obligation

Help for the poor, which historically has been a bedrock object of philanthropy, has been largely preempted by government in recent decades. This has happened not so much because parallel public agencies have moved in to take the place of traditional private social service agencies, though such a supplanting has occurred to some degree. More significantly, immense new programs have been launched and expanded in recent decades that have altered society's whole institutional structure for, and attitude about, dealing with the problems of the poor. One observation in a study on the Community Service Society of New York City illustrates the profound shift that has taken place. In the depression year of 1931, the study notes, more than one third of what was spent for relief in the city was privately contributed, principally by a charitable organization with the now quaint sounding name of the Association for Improving Conditions of the Poor. The association has since merged into the Community Service Society and it spends far more than it did back in the thirties, mainly on research, education and community organization projects. But the conditions of the poor in New York City in the recession

91

year of 1975 depended overwhelmingly on massive government outlays under multibillion-dollar welfare and social insurance programs.

The Great Drepression was the epochal spur to this change. "The depression," writes historian Robert Bremner, "shattered the myth that private charity could tide the deserving poor over bad times." And in so doing, it became the impetus for shifting help for the poor from an essentially private, "charitable" concern to a government responsibility, from dependence on the beneficence of private organizations and individuals to a society-wide entitlement to at least a bare minimum standard of living.

As a result of the ravages of the depression, Congress passed the Social Security Act of 1935, which is the basis for a whole range of federal and state assistance and income-support programs, for the poor, the unemployed, the aged, the infirm—in sum, the main beneficiaries of traditional "philanthropy." F. Emerson Andrews has described the Social Security Act as "the largest single stride ever made in bringing into the orbit of government those services that were formerly first charges on private philanthropy."

Some measure of the enormous impact of Social Security legislation can be seen in arithmetic such as this:

—In 1929, old-age, survivors, disability and health insurance did not exist at all. In 1950, some $784 million was spent under this program, which is what most people think of when they say Social Security. In fiscal 1974, more than $66 billion was dispensed.

—In 1929, $60 million was spent by government on various forms of assistance—what is generally known as "welfare." In fiscal 1974, the amount was more than $25 billion.

—Private philanthropy, by comparison, distributed in 1974 around $2.3 billion in the whole "social welfare" category, according to estimates by the American Association of Fund-Raising Counsel.

The predominance of government in health, education, and most dramatic of all, welfare, has been regretted and resisted at one stage or another by various groups within the nonprofit world. On the other hand, this development can be and has been looked upon as part of a process that reflects one of the abiding virtues of the nonprofit sector.

Earlier parts of this report have noted the "pioneering" role of nonprofit activity and the fact that in some areas, this pioneering has, in effect, moved the activity beyond private philanthropy's capacity for sustained subsidization. The process is described by David Owen in his observations on English philanthropy, observations that would appear to apply to American philanthropy equally as well. Philanthropy, Owen wrote, was central in shedding light on the dimensions of a social problem or growing public want, but having done so, it often proved unable by itself to solve the problem or fulfill the want. "As soon as the terms of the problem were accurately defined," he found, "it was seen to lie well beyond the scope of voluntary agencies." In more concrete terms, the director of Atlanta's United Way, asked by a Commission reporter what the major pending problems of that city were, answered health, youth guidance, emergency funds, day care and remedial care—all of which were once considered to be principally the concerns of voluntary organizations. "But," he said, "because of our limited funds, we just can't touch them. They're too big for us." A report on philanthropy in the Cleveland area takes note, in the same vein, of "the arithmetic growth of private sector funding in its attempts to meet the geometric growth of public needs."

As certain minimal levels of health, education and welfare have increasingly come to be regarded as broad social needs to be attended to as rights of citizenship rather than as benefits charitably and selectively bestowed, the state has emerged as the appropriate agency to oversee and allocate resources in these areas. The point is illustrated in a book called The Welfare State published two decades ago, in which it is pointed out that The New York Times' annual appeal for contributions to the "Hundred Neediest Cases" was published in the London Times in 1952, accompanied by the commentary that in England only ten of the 100 would have had to depend on private help. Ninety would have had a claim to the help they needed as a matter of right under one government program or another. Possibly these days almost as many Americans from that old Hundred Neediest list would find their needs answered by

93

the current array of government health and welfare programs.

Should government help for the poor continue to change in a direction that it appears to be moving, there would be even less central a role for private aid. This thrust is not toward helping the poor per se but toward ridding society of poverty. And eliminating poverty is increasingly seen as a matter of redistributing income and wealth. What the poor need most of all, according to this viewpoint, are neither charitable services, governmental equivalents nor even assurances of minimal standards of health, education and welfare, but money.

We are still a long way from guaranteed minimum incomes for all Americans of course. But a move in this direction was incorporated in the 1975 tax reduction measure—a small step toward a negative income tax, under which people below certain income levels receive government income supplements instead of paying taxes. If a full-scale income maintenance system evolves, the roles of nonprofit organizations that are now still mainly concerned with helping the poor will presumably change further. It is safe to assume, however, that there will always be an important role for nonprofit groups to play in filling the gaps, sometimes sizable ones—at the local level, among special groups, involving unrecognized problems—which the broad, often undiscriminating reach of governmental programs and operations probably will always leave in aiding the unable or the unfortunate of society.

Government Financial Assistance

If a major effect on the growth of the welfare state has been to lessen the need for some philanthropic functions, it is clear that many of these functions—and attendant organizations—remain. Schools, colleges and universities, hospitals and art institutions appear to be as indispensable as ever. Government expansions in these areas have not involved major institutional changes so much as simply helping to pay the bills. This help is not, it should be clear, for propping up organizations for the sake of their own institutional survival; it reflects a politically arrived at determination that nonprofit organizations to or

94

through which public funds flow provide important public benefits to the direct users of the organizations' services, ultimately to society as a whole.

Among the many government programs that have sprung up in recent decades to provide substantial public support for nonprofit activities are the following:

—The school lunch program, which reimburses private (as well as public) schools for lunches served.

—Headstart grants, for preschool programs for poor children.

—Donation of surplus properties to health and educational institutions.

—Mortgage insurance for cooperative nonprofit housing construction, acquisition or rehabilitation.

—Lease or acquisition by nonprofit associations or corporations of public lands for recreation, historical monuments or other public purposes.

—Grants for building hospitals and for other health-related construction, The Hill-Burton Program, which spurred the construction of hundreds of voluntary hospitals.

—A program that provides full-time workers, paid by government, for community projects (VISTA).

—Preferential postal rates, under which nonprofit organizations can save as much as 73 per cent on mailing costs.

This sampling only includes benefits or subsidies that go directly to nonprofit organizations to help support the services they render to the public. At least as important in some areas are government programs that help users of nonprofit services, users who might not be able to afford these services otherwise. Among these programs are medical allowances for the elderly and the poor (Medicare and Medicaid), which have become major factors in the finances of voluntary hospitals. Federal and state scholarship aid has likewise become integral to the support of private colleges and universities. Indeed, ever since enactment of the GI Bill, student aid has been the principal vehicle of federal support for higher education; it now accounts for more than 73 cents of every dollar of federal support to higher education, or around $4 billion as of 1973.

Dilemma Over Control and Finances

This ever increasing amount of involvement by government in the finances of nonprofit organizations presents a dilemma for the nonprofit sector. On the one hand, government money is needed—is a matter of life or death for many organizations—as the number and size of nonprofit groups has grown and the amount of private funding has, in recent years, moved relatively slowly and even fallen off as measured in deflated dollars. On the other hand, government money obviously comes with strings attached, however invisible and unintentional they may be. The more a private nonprofit organization depends on government money for survival, the less "private" it is going to be, the less immune to the influence of public political processes and priorities.

All the same, government support for much nonprofit activity is an indisputable fact of life that must be lived with and reckoned with. The nonprofit sector has become an increasingly mixed realm, part private, part public, in much the same sense that the profit-making sector has—and not unlike the nonprofit sector itself once was. As the Commission's historical survey points out, when it came to attending to public purposes, the lines between public and private resources and agencies were much less sharply drawn in earlier American history than they have been in recent decades. In colonial days, when public funds were low, public overseers of the poor would call on the churches for special collections of alms. Early philanthropists often gave or bequeathed money to government for charitable purposes. At the same time, private organizations frequently received government money without practical or ideological qualms. Harvard University, like many of America's first colleges and universities, started out with government assistance, £400 from the General Court of Massachusetts, as well as private, £400 and a library from John Harvard. Throughout the nineteenth century, too, it was not uncommon for states and cities to subsidize privately run schools, orphan homes, juvenile reformatories, hospitals and institutions for the handicapped.

Although this practice of public support for private nonprofit organizations and the public services they provided was commonplace, it was also subject to frequent criticism. And the lines between public and private services and support sharpened over time. So if the lines are beginning to blur again, it is in a context of a certain mutual wariness. The burgeoning size of government underlies and may even have intensified in recent decades an uneasiness in voluntary areas over public support. One survey for the Commission appears to reflect this unease. It found that among a sampling of voluntary sector leaders, government-voluntary relations were the foremost concern of those questioned.

Seeking a Balance

A perfect balance between a level of government control, which inevitably accompanies government financial support, and sufficient autonomy by the nonprofit beneficiary is perhaps unattainable. But various methods aimed at approaching a balance are emerging as the nonprofit sector's dependence on public support grows.

Several federal and state funding organizations have sprung up in recent years which are appropriated sums to dispense within nonprofit areas, agencies such as the National Endowment for the Arts, the National Endowment for the Humanities, the National Institutes of Health, the Corporation for Public Broadcasting and various state arts councils. Insulated from daily politics, they operate somewhat like private philanthropic foundations, although they are periodically accountable to, and dependent on, legislatures for new funds, which makes them more susceptible to political priorities than are private foundations. In usual governmental fashion, for instance, they are inclined to approximate an equal geographical distribution of grants regardless of more intrinsic merits of grantees. Still, within such limits, these "insulated" institutions seem generally to have played a valuable role. In the arts, where government aid is relatively new, these institutions account for the great bulk of public support, and their funding has been at least as beneficial, in some eyes, as some private sources of support.

Another approach to government funding of nonprofit services that is already widely used in some areas is to subsidize users of services rather than directly fund the services themselves. As noted above, the bulk of federal spending in higher education is in the form of aid to students rather than to educational institutions. In theory, at least, such aid does not involve the government as directly in the policies of institutions, beyond setting broad guidelines as to what organizations qualify for user aid.

A greatly expanded program of tuition aid, aimed at narrowing the growing gap between public and private tuitions in higher education, was proposed in early 1975 by the Carnegie Council on Policy Studies in Higher Education. Under the Council's plan, "tuition equalization grants" of $750 a year would be paid to students, half the money coming from the federal government, half from the states. This is the latest of numerous proposals for tuition subsidies. At the pre-college level, similar proposals have been suggested for supplying credits, "vouchers," to students who would then be free to spend them—at public or private schools—as they see fit. This method is seen as the potential salvation of hard-pressed private schools and colleges, especially those with religious affiliations which the courts have decreed to be constitutionally barred from forms of direct governmental aid. Yet all such proposals have run into heavy opposition from public education leaders, who see student subsidies for private education as a threat to public education systems.

As many studies made for the Commission suggest, perhaps the most effective, and most possible, insulation of all from purse-string control is to have more than one purse to draw from. A private organization may be totally reliant on public support and, if the organization's activities, the social conditions and the institutional arrangements are right, still maintain a significant degree of autonomy. But memories of loyalty oaths as a condition of government funding still are fresh, as are recollections that the institutions that resisted such pressures had private as well as governmental resources to draw on.

Moreover, as Chapter II notes, the day-to-day attitudes of those who direct and staff nonprofit organizations are likely to exhibit more independence if they have a source of funds that is not subject to official or legislative review. The presence of a firm core of private support, however small, in a private organization that gets major public funding can be of crucial importance in determining whether the managers of the organization regard themselves and behave as independent operators or as civil servants. The importance of private support, in other words, may be at least as great in a mixed nonprofit sector as in a purely private one, even if this importance may be, at times, more subtle.

Private support itself, however, it must be recognized, does not fall outside the mixture of public and private influences. The amounts, sources and recipients of private giving are affected by government through the tax laws. Indeed, because private giving is so basic to the independence of the nonprofit sector, government's influence on giving—which is by no means neutral—poses some of the major issues to be resolved in the broad and broadening intermix between the third sector and government.

Sources for Chapter IV

Robert J. Blendon, *The Changing Role of Private Philanthropy in Health Affairs.**

Daniel P. Bourque, *Private Foundations and Federal Government Support for Education and Education-Related Activities, Fiscal Year 1973*, The National Planning Association, Washington, D.C.*

Blair T. Bower, *The Role of Private Philanthropy in Relation to Environment—Pollution.**

Gerard M. Brannon and James Strnad, *Alternative Approaches to Encouraging Philanthropic Activities.**

Robert H. Bremner, *Private Philanthropy and Public Needs: An Historical Perspective.**

John J. Carson and Harry V. Hodson, eds., *Philanthropy in the '70's: An Anglo-American Discussion*, Council on Foundations, Inc., New York, 1973.

Earl F. Cheit and Theodore E. Lobman III, *Philanthropy and Higher Education.**

Bice Clemow, *Search for the Bridge: The Stand-off Between City Hall and "Five Points" in Atlanta.**

Wilbur J. Cohen, *Some Aspects of Evolving Social Policy in Relation to Private Philanthropy.**

Commission on Foundations and Private Philanthropy, *Foundations, Private Giving and Public Policy*, University of Chicago Press, Chicago, 1970.

Committee on the Law and Practice Relating to Charitable Trusts (Nathan Committee), *Report on Charitable Trusts*, Her Majesty's Stationery Office, London, 1952.

Fred R. Crawford, *Non-Economic Motivational Factors in Philanthropic Behavior.**

Donald A. Erickson, *Philanthropy, Public Needs and Nonpublic Schools.**

Solomon Fabricant, "Philanthropy in the American Economy," *Foundation News*, Vol. X., No. 5, September-October 1969.

Caryl P. Haskins, *The Role of Private Philanthropy and Public Support of Science in the United States.**

Caroline Hightower, *A Report on the Arts.**

Hans H. Jenny, *Philanthropy in Higher Education.**

C. Harry Kahn, *Personal Deductions in the Federal Income Tax*, Princeton University Press, Princeton, 1960.

Eric Larrabee, *The Public Funding Agency.**

Reynold Levy and Waldemar A. Nielsen, *An Agenda for the Future.**

Robert S. Merriman, *Cleveland: Faint Halo Around a Solid Tradition of Giving.**

National Center for Voluntary Action, *A Report on Voluntary Activities and Leadership Opinion.**

David Owen, *English Philanthropy, 1660-1960*, Harvard University Press, Cambridge, 1964.

John P. Persons, John J. Osborn, Jr. and Charles F. Feldman, *Criteria for Exemption Under Section 501(c)(3).**

Alfred M. Skolnik and Sophie R. Dales, "Social Welfare Expenditures, Fiscal 1974," in *Social Security Bulletin*, January, 1975.

United States Government, *Listing of Selected Federal Aid Available Exclusively to Nonprofit Organizations and Institutions*, 1975.

United States Human Resources Corporation, *Foundations' Responsiveness to Concerns of Minority Groups*, San Francisco, 1975.

Joseph L. Vigilante and Ruth Kantrow, *The Voluntary Social Agency Experiments, Innovates, Demonstrates, and Influences Public Social Policy: The Community Service Society of New York 1930-1970.**

Laurens Williams and Donald V. Moorehead, *An Analysis of the Federal Tax Distinctions Between Public and Private Charitable Organizations.**

Ellen Winston, *Some Aspects of Private Philanthropy in Relation to Social Welfare.**

Paul N. Ylvisaker and Jane H. Mavity, *The Role of Private Philanthropy in Public Affairs.**

*Denotes reports and studies undertaken for the Commission.

V

TAXES AND NONTAXES

As long as there have been taxes, governments have been able to influence giving and nonprofit activity by the ways in which they have levied, or not levied, imposts on donor, donation or donee. The power of taxation has been used at times in other lands to undermine nonprofit institutions and associations. But the predominant pattern throughout American history has been one of growing governmental encouragement of private giving and nonprofit organization through the tax laws.

The Spread of Nontaxation

This encouragement has developed in the United States primarily through a broadening and deepening of immunities from taxation. Such immunities reflect an underlying quid pro quo—the belief that society is well compensated for tax revenues foregone because the activities and services thereby aided and encouraged are of benefit to society. A frequently cited justification for tax immunities that affect nonprofit organizations is that government, in fact, would itself have to supply many of the services, fill many of the functions, of such organizations if they did not exist.

Exemption from property taxes is one of the principal immunities enjoyed by nonprofit organizations and also one of the oldest. Following English precedents, such exemptions have been accorded in America to religious and educational organizations since colonial days. Secular charitable institutions expanded in number and generally became exempt from property taxes in the nineteenth century. Today, every state has some form of property tax exemption for nonprofit organizations, and exempt private nonprofit property encompasses no less than one ninth of all property in the United States, it is estimated, and accounts for some $5 billion a year in unlevied tax revenues.

Religious, educational, charitable and scientific organizations have been exempt from federal income taxes, too, ever since today's basic income tax law was enacted in 1913. Certain kinds of nonprofit organizations are exempt from certain other federal taxes as well. Nonprofit educational organizations do not have to pay excise taxes on purchases of items for their exclusive use. Nonprofit hospitals and some nonprofit educational organizations are exempt from federal taxes on telephone services. Charitable "drawings" are exempt from the 10 per cent federal tax on wagers.

But possibly the single largest tax immunity benefiting the nonprofit sector is a provision of the federal tax laws that applies not to nonprofit organizations directly but to those who give to eligible nonprofit groups and institutions—the "charitable deduction" from personal income taxes. Under this provision, the taxpayer can subtract a "charitable" donation from his or her income before calculating the tax to be paid. Like the tax exemption, the tax deduction has expanded in scope over the years. Only 15 per cent of a person's income was deductible when the charitable deduction was enacted in 1917. This was increased to 20 per cent in 1952, to 30 per cent for certain types of nonprofit organizations in 1954, to 50 per cent for more kinds in 1969. In 1974, approximately 30 million people used the charitable deduction, thereby reducing the amount of federal income taxes they otherwise would have paid by around $4 billion and, as Commission studies referred to later in this report indicate, increasing their giving to nonprofit organizations by at least as much.

The long-range trend, in other words, has been one of general expansion of tax immunity for the sake of nonprofit activity. A study of tax laws in other countries indicates that such immunity has become of far greater significance in size and scope in the United States than in any other nation. So deeply rooted is this practice in American ways, in fact, that it would appear to enjoy almost constitutional status in many Americans' eyes. (Nontaxation of religious organizations is held by

104

some legal authorities to be literally prescribed by the Constitution under the 1st Amendment prohibition against laws "respecting an establishment of religion.")

Countermovements

These are times, however, as this report notes elsewhere, in which many institutions and institutional arrangements in our society are being reexamined, and the degree and pattern of nontaxation of charitable organizations and of philanthropic giving is clearly among them. Indeed, nontaxation serves as a convenient, concrete focus for social concerns that have probably always been a counterpoint to the admiration and praise directed at philanthropic giving; nontaxation serves as a focus in particular for a frequently evidenced wariness about the relationship of private giving to personal and institutional wealth and power, a wariness that may well be growing in this day of heightened social sensitivities and broadening egalitarian sentiments.

In any case, there have been a number of signs in recent years that tax immunities benefiting nonprofit organizations may no longer be generally considered above questioning. Among the signs is the fact that a number of communities in the past decade have attempted to exact property taxes or "voluntary" payments in lieu of taxes from exempt organizations that use public services but have not had to pay for them. Mounting property tax rates to meet straining municipal budgets have been a major impetus to such challenges to the property tax exemption. "As is true with any tax source," a Commission report on tax exemption bluntly puts it, "the higher the rate the more difficult to grant a free ride . . ."

There has been greater scrutiny of the income of tax-exempt organizations, too, in recent years; income that flows from enterprises that are run by, but are not directly related to the purposes of, tax-exempt entities is now subject to taxation. At the federal level, the four per cent "auditing fee" tax on foundation income that was enacted in 1969 is viewed by some mainly as reflecting Congress's unhappiness with foundations, but others glimpse a much broader implication, a precedent.

105

CHALLENGING THE CHARITABLE
DEDUCTION

Potentially the most serious challenge to the system of tax immunities affecting nonprofit activity concerns—directly and indirectly—the charitable deduction under the federal personal income tax, which influences by far the largest source of private giving to nonprofit organizations, giving by individuals.

The income tax deduction was enacted just four years after the income tax itself became a permanent fixture of American life. The deduction was part of the Second Revenue Act of 1917, which steeply boosted income tax rates to help pay for America's entry into World War I. The main tax principle, or philosophy, that was articulated in support of the deduction at that time was the contention that the income tax should be imposed only on consumable income, that the government should not tax the portion of a person's income that is devoted to charity, which was seen as going to public uses and not to the giver's personal advantage or enrichment. The "income definition" viewpoint remains the principal philosophical rationale for the charitable deduction today, and it is subscribed to by a number of economists and tax experts.

The charitable deduction was enacted not only or even primarily as a matter of tax philosophy, however, but because of hard practical considerations. It was feared that in reducing disposable income, the new steep income tax rates would cause upper-income donors to cut back on their contributions to institutions that depended on such gifts. Senator H. F. Hollis, one of the authors of legislation enacting the charitable deduction pronounced this viewpoint in introducing the bill. People, he said, usually "contribute to charities and educational objects out of their surplus . . . Now, when war comes and we impose these very heavy taxes on incomes, that will be the first place where the wealthy men will be tempted to economize . . . They will say, 'Charity begins at home.' "

The need for private philanthropic funds to support major nonprofit organizations remains today the main pragmatic basis for the charitable deduction, accompanying the philosophical basis of the "income definition" rationale. Among the challenges confronting the charitable deduction is the fact that both bases are today being questioned.

Philosophical Challenge

A major challenge to the philosophical basis of the charitable deduction lies in the contention that charitable giving is not that different from other kinds of personal outlays and therefore should not be treated differently under the income tax. This viewpoint is summarized in a study for the Commission by Paul R. McDaniel of Boston College Law School. ". . . Most economists and social psychologists," he writes, "take the 'scientific' view that charitable contributions are not simply individual sacrifices for the public good, but are actually consumption spending . . . In making a charitable gift, the individual is seen as purchasing status, the perpetuation of his social values, or on a less mercenary level, the satisfaction resulting from doing a 'good deed.' . . . And one can inquire as to whether the deduction operates equitably as an incentive system to induce this form of consumption."

Overlapping this argument in recent years has been the more vigorous and somewhat less abstract contention of tax reformers that the charitable deduction is not distinct from a number of other deductions that have been built into the income tax, and that all of them are wanting by the yardstick of equity.

According to this viewpoint, all tax immunities are forms of government subsidy to whatever activity benefits from nontaxation. This is not a new idea. A president of Harvard University, Charles William Eliot, acknowledged and attacked this way of looking at tax immunity a century ago. "It has been often asserted," he said, "that to exempt an institution from taxation is the same thing as to grant it money directly from the public treasury. This statement is sophistical and fallacious." But the

107

tax-immunity-as-subsidy viewpoint has gained considerable influence among tax analysts in recent years. It was adopted by the federal government in 1968 when the Treasury Secretary's annual report included a "tax expenditure" section. This section lists the amounts by which the government is seen to be subsidizing various areas through forms of nontaxation or reduced taxes. In the federal budget for fiscal 1976, $91.8 billion was the total estimated for tax expenditures, including $4.84 billion attributed to the personal income tax charitable deduction (fourth on the list after deductions for state and local taxes, for home mortgage interest costs and for pension contributions).

Nor is the tax expenditure viewpoint limited to tax analysts or government ledgers. A ghetto activist in Hartford who challenges the pattern of corporation and foundation philanthropy in that city was quick to evoke the viewpoint during an interview for a Commission report. His position: "These corporations and foundations are tax exempt. Therefore, part of the money they spend is my money. Therefore, they should have regulatory restrictions placed upon them that will force them to meet specific social criteria . . ." The result of one foundation's practices, he charged later, was "to use charitable giving—a form of federal subsidy—to perpetuate the effects of past discrimination."

When seen as a form of government subsidy or expenditure, the charitable deduction, like other personal income tax deductions, is open to charges of inequity because of a pattern that is, in effect, the inverse of the progressive structure of the income tax. The higher a person's income the higher the rate of taxation under the income tax and therefore the more the government foregoes—or "spends" in the tax-expenditure view—for any portion of such income not taxed. In other words, the government adds proportionately more of the subsidy to a high-income taxpayer's giving and proportionately less to the low-income taxpayer's contribution.

Stanley S. Surrey of Harvard Law School, formerly Assistant Secretary of the Treasury for Tax Policy, is the foremost proponent of this way of looking at tax deductions, starting with his advocacy of a tax-expenditure budget while he was in the

Treasury Department. Talking of the charitable deduction in a Commission discussion, Surrey illustrated the tax-expenditure viewpoint in this way:

"Let us look at this subsidy to charities which is given by the charitable deduction. Well, it was a very peculiar subsidy. It's sort of an upside-down affair. As you know, if a person in the 70 per cent bracket gives a sum of money, he is able to deduct that sum of money from his tax base, and in effect he is only giving 30 per cent, whereas when a person in the 14 per cent bracket gives a sum of money, he is giving 86 per cent. Or to put it differently, if a $200,000 person gives 10 per cent of his income to charity, it really costs the government $14,000 to get $6,000 out of that person . . . If a $12,000 person gives 10 per cent of his income to charity, it costs the government $324 to get $876 from this person. The charitable deduction works just upside down."

In a recent attack on what he described as the disproportionate benefit to high-income taxpayers of tax expenditures in general, Senator Walter Mondale included the charitable deduction and calculated what the effect of the deduction, from the tax-expenditure viewpoint, looks like in aggregate terms. Some $3.8 billion in tax expenditures, he figured, were accounted for by the charitable deduction in fiscal 1974 (his calculations put contributions to education in a separate category). Of this, 66.7 per cent went to families with adjusted gross incomes of more than $20,000, representing 14.6 per cent of all taxpayers. "The concentration of tax expenditure benefits in the higher income brackets," said Mondale, "is one of the important reasons these provisions must be examined with great care. If the federal government is, in effect, going to be spending money to support or reward certain activities, we must determine whether it makes sense to do so under a system which provides the highest benefits to those with the highest incomes."

The tax-expenditure viewpoint and its implications are by no means universally accepted. A major argument that has been raised against the whole notion of tax "expenditures" is that it implies that all income covered by tax laws is government money. It is only in this light, it is contended, that non-

109

taxation can be seen as a subsidy or expenditure.

The equity implications of the tax-expenditure viewpoint are also challenged by those who argue that the alleged disparity of tax expenditures in favor of high-income taxpayers is merely the mirrored reflection of the progressive income tax, which is structured against them. In other words, nontaxation of portions of higher incomes because of tax exemptions or deductions is only higher, can only be viewed as a greater government expenditure, because the tax rates are set higher for upper-income levels to begin with.

Perhaps the principal counter-argument to the tax-expenditure viewpoint as far as its application to the charitable deduction goes rests with the "income definition" rationale for the deduction. According to this reasoning, tax allowances for philanthropic giving cannot be looked at or measured in the same way as tax privileges for other purposes because money given to charity is not an element of income that should be subject to government's taxing power to begin with. Boris I. Bittker of Yale Law School posed the "income-definition" argument against the "tax-expenditure" viewpoint this way in the same Commission discussion in which Stanley Surrey took part:

". . . The concept of income is not settled, cannot be settled the way one can define water as H_2O or lay down the laws of gravity . . . Income is a political, economic, social concept which takes its meaning from the society in which the term is used, in my view. And there are many definitions of income . . . But at the very core of the only definition that has the benefit of a consensus, there is a concept of consumption . . . I would assert that consumption certainly consists of what one spends on food, shelter and clothing for himself, his family, friends, what one saves to pass on to heirs and so on . . . But 2,000 years of religious, philosophical and ethical views suggest that what one gives to charity can properly be viewed differently . . . If, as I think, we have a powerful sense of difference between giving to charity and spending in other respects, I see no reason at all why in defining income one shouldn't exclude those items like charitable contributions that our whole history tells us represent a special kind of use of one's funds."

Yet another view that the Commission heard expressed by

110

tax experts was that those who support the charitable deduction should have no argument with the tax-expenditure viewpoint, but should be willing to view tax savings from the charitable deduction as a form of tax expenditure and simply assert that, for special reasons associated with philanthropic giving, it was a desirable form of tax expenditure, whereas other forms were not necessarily desirable. This view in turn has been challenged on the grounds that to regard charitable tax savings as a form of government expenditure is to undermine the "income definition" case for the deduction, because it means conceding that the charitable deduction is not fundamentally different from other deductions and allowances.

The pros and cons of the tax-expenditure viewpoint continue to be argued, often heatedly, as do its implications for the charitable and other deductions. Meanwhile, however, the viewpoint seems to be taking an ever firmer hold within government. The tax-expenditure part of the Treasury Secretary's report was instituted in 1968 by administrative decision. In 1974, Congress wrote the tax-expenditure viewpoint into law: it passed legislation requiring that as of 1975 a tax-expenditure section be included in the federal budget. In all likelihood, tax exemptions, deductions, credits—including those benefiting nonprofit organizations—will be increasingly scrutinized by Congress as if they were forms of government spending, whatever the implications.

Pragmatic Doubts

Alongside of, and perhaps fueling, the philosophical challenge to the charitable deduction, its logic and its equity, have been doubts, perhaps growing ones, about the pragmatic basis of the deduction—about the need for the deduction in order to maintain essential organizations and services.

That the deduction was needed to maintain giving levels and that this giving was essential to the survival of certain major institutions was evidently little questioned when the charitable deduction was instituted in 1917, nor was the public benefit derived from those institutions questioned. Recurrently

111

since then, however, the assumed effectiveness of the charitable deduction as a stimulus to giving has been doubted by experts and by political leaders. And in recent years, as private giving has become a shrinking element in the support of traditional objects of philanthropy, the need for this giving has become a more subtle and in some eyes may appear to be a less compelling proposition.

Meantime the nation has moved from vigorous growth to an economy of high unemployment and inflation. Public budgets have been severely strained in recent years. So the public benefit derived from objects of philanthropy probably tends these days to be regarded in relative more than in absolute terms, to be weighed—along with the tax costs of philanthropy—against other public benefits including those that have been eliminated or restricted because of government budget cutbacks.

Cases in recent years in which some prominent well-to-do Americans have paid little or no taxes in support of governmental services, in part because of deductions taken for charitable giving, have put governmental versus philanthropic priorities on the scales in a dramatic and highly publicized way that has probably not enhanced public sympathies for the philanthropic priorities. Observations by the then ranking Republican member of the House Ways and Means Committee, Rep. John Byrnes, made in the course of the 1969 tax reform hearings, reflect this probability. "The real problem here," he said, "is that certain people have a choice as to how the tax aspect of their income is going to be spent. Others have to let the government say how it is going to be spent . . . And they must also pay a higher price because some people with wealth have said they do not want to support any of these governmental services." "I feel that people who enjoy wealth . . . should be encouraged to engage in more philanthropy," he went on. "But when the incentive is given to use moneys [for philanthropy] that otherwise would be going toward the payment of Government services, and when we don't suffer from an excess of that money, then perhaps our encouragement is misplaced . . ."

Is governmental encouragement of philanthropy through the charitable deduction misplaced? This Commission does not think so, for reasons that are discussed in the next chapter of this report. Yet apart from the merit or lack of merit underlying such skepticism, the very fact that it was voiced by a moderate and influential member of Congress is an indication that government encouragement of philanthropy may no longer be—if it ever was—politically invulnerable simply because of its association with the cause of philanthropy.

Standard Deduction vs. Charitable Deduction

In fact, the charitable deduction has already proved in recent years to be highly vulnerable to at least indirect political erosion. Such erosion has taken place of late as a result of the expansion of the "standard deduction." Since 1944, all taxpayers have had the option of deducting from their income for tax computation purposes a set amount or a proportion of their income as an alternative to adding up all the separate deductions allowable to them—for home mortgage payments, local and state taxes, medical expenses and so forth, including gifts to charity. Those who take the standard deduction can effect an appreciable tax savings, but because no actual outlays need be made to take the standard deduction, such savings do not act as an inducement to any particular form of expenditure. Standard deductors, in other words, feel no inducements from specific deductions, including the charitable deduction.

Understandably, the standard deduction's effect on the charitable deduction has been a matter of concern to the world of philanthropy since 1944; but it tended to become less worrisome for many years as "itemizers," those who did not take the standard deduction, rapidly grew in proportion to those who did. Partly as a result of expanding home ownership, accompanied by a growing number of taxpayers with mortgage interest payments to deduct, the number of itemizers increased from less than one fifth (18 per cent) of all taxpayers soon after the standard deduction was enacted to nearly half (48 per cent) in 1970. But since then, the level of the standard deduction has increased, and so has the proportion of standard deductors. In 1972, only 35 per cent of taxpayers itemized their deductions. A further increase of the standard deduction for 1975 returns

113

was expected to reduce those taking separate deductions—including the charitable deduction—to 31 per cent of all taxpayers.

This constricting of the reach of the charitable deduction in terms of the number of taxpayers affected both reflects and may further fuel political challenges to government's major encouragement to giving. On the one hand, it signifies that the charitable deduction is, along with other deductions, given a lower political priority than tax simplicity and easing the tax burden on lower incomes—which are among the main purposes behind higher standard deductions. At the same time, as fewer and fewer Americans avail themselves of the charitable deduction, this tax provision's constituency may be narrowed, its political underpinning weakened.

Such are some of the challenges, conceptual and concrete, social and economic—all having ultimate political implications —which the Commission finds to be confronting the charitable deduction as our society's principal institutional encouragement to philanthropic giving. This is not to say that such giving itself is being challenged or that the objects and purposes of such giving are being challenged. Nor are the viewpoints or trends that present the challenges by any means immune to change and challenge themselves. Indeed, in the following chapter, the Commission offers from its own research and expertise what it feels are powerful reasons for maintaining the charitable deduction, whatever its defects may be. At the same time, the Commission feels that the challenges to the charitable deduction, however valid or invalid their premises or purposes might be, cannot be ignored by the nonprofit sector.

They are, therefore, viewed as part of the contemporary context in which the Commission addresses itself to recommendations involving the changing course of American philanthropy and the nonprofit sector. These recommendations, and the weighings and further findings behind them, are the subject of Part II of this report, which follows.

Sources for Chapter V

Arthur Andersen & Co., *Overview of Governmental Support and Financial Regulation of Philanthropic Organizations in Selected Nations.**

William D. Andrews, "Personal Deductions in an Ideal Income Tax," *Harvard Law Review*, Vol. 86, No. 2, December, 1972.

Chauncey Belknap and Philip Mandel, *The Federal Income Tax Exemption of Charitable Organizations: Its History and Underlying Policy*, Rockefeller Foundation, New York, 1954.

Boris I. Bittker and Stanley S. Surrey, *Philanthropy and the Tax System*, Commission Discussion, January 15, 1974.**

Landrum R. Bolling, *Statement Submitted to the Subcommittee on Foundations of the Senate Finance Committee*, June 1974.

Gerard M. Brannon and James Strnad, *Alternative Approaches to Encouraging Philanthropic Activities.**

George F. Break, *Charitable Contributions Under the Federal Individual Income Tax: Alternative Policy Options.**

John J. Carson and Harry V. Hodson, eds., *Philanthropy in the '70's: An Anglo-American Discussion*, Council on Foundations, Inc., New York, 1973.

Vivian Gornick, *Money Above, Action Below: Philanthropy in Hartford.**

C. Harry Kahn, *Personal Deductions in the Federal Income Tax*, Princeton University Press, Princeton, 1960.

Irving Kristol, "Taxes, Poverty and Equality," in *The Public Interest*, Fall, 1974.

Julian H. Levi, *Financing Education and the Effect of the Tax Laws.**

Paul R. McDaniel, *Study of Federal Matching Grants for Charitable Contributions.**

National Center for Voluntary Action, *A Report on Voluntary Activities and Leadership Opinion.**

John P. Persons, John J. Osborn Jr. and Charles F. Feldman, *Criteria for Exemption Under Section 501(c)(3).**

John F. Shannon and L. Richard Gabler, *The Exemption of Religious, Educational and Charitable Institutions from Property Taxation.**

U.S. House of Representatives, Ways and Means Committee, *Hearings on Tax Treatment of Charitable Contributions*, February 27, 1969.

U.S. Senate, Report of Proceedings, Subcommittee on Foundations, Committee on Finance, *Impact of Current Economic Crisis on Foundations and Recipients of Foundation Money*, November 25, 1974.

William Vickrey, "Private Philanthropy and Public Finance," in *Altruism, Morality and Economic Theory*, Edmund S. Phelps, ed., Russell Sage Foundation, New York, 1975.

Richard E. Wagner, *Death, Taxes and Charitable Bequests: A Survey of Issues and Options.**

John A. Wallace and Robert W. Fisher, *The Income Tax Deduction for Charitable Contributions by Individuals.**

Laurens Williams and Donald V. Moorehead, *An Analysis of the Federal Tax Distinctions Between Public and Private Charitable Organizations.**

*Denotes reports and studies undertaken for the Commission.

PART II
TOWARD A STRONGER VOLUNTARY SECTOR

Conclusions and Recommendations
of the Commission

INTRODUCTION TO PART II

At this point in its report, the Commission turns to specific recommendations aimed at strengthening and improving the structures and processes of the voluntary sector, recommendations that are aimed ultimately at increasing the benefits, direct and indirect, material and spiritual, that the sector provides society. These recommendations are based on a number of broad conclusions by the Commission about this area of American life, about changes and challenges to established patterns within this area, and about continuities as well.

The Commission feels that the data and expert opinion and analysis it has consulted, as summarized in the previous chapters, affirms that the "third sector" plays a large and vital role in American life, especially important today as a counterbalance to the giant institutions of society's other two sectors—business and government. The third sector provides, in effect, an arena within which the individual, often a barely visible or audible force in today's society, can exercise personal initiative toward the betterment of his community or of the nation or humankind as a whole.

Far more significant in size and scope than in any other country, the third sector's array of private nonprofit organizations also reflects a deeply rooted American tenet which has been reinforced by recent tremors in the nation's governance—the conviction that no single institutional structure should exercise a monopoly on filling public needs, that a reliance on government alone to fill such needs not only saps the spirit of individual initiative but risks making human values subservient to institutional ones, individual and community purposes to bureaucratic conveniences or authoritarian dictates.

The evidence presented to the Commission and the experience of many Commission members themselves also indicates that private support is an essential underpinning of nonprofit organizations, that the autonomy of such organizations clearly depends on private contributions of money and labor and that the pluralistic value of third sector organizations depends on a high level of autonomy. Although greater public funding of

119

many traditional nonprofit services appears inevitable as one of the on-going changes affecting the voluntary sector, the very fact of an alternative source of support can preserve a significant degree of independence in outlook and control in a publicly funded "private" organization that might otherwise become indistinguishable from a government agency.

The Commission believes that government must not try to solve all our problems. The great strength of our society has been individual initiative, which has long been reflected in Americans' tendency to pursue common goals through voluntary organizations and associations. Philanthropy, a means, not an end in itself, is a way of exercising and supporting such initiative to make possible alternatives to government, to supplement government efforts and to help assure the maintenance of a pluralistic society.

The Commission feels, therefore, that the level of philanthropic giving must be increased if giving and nonprofit activity are to continue to play major roles in American life. Not only do many specific nonprofit causes depend for their autonomy on such support and many beneficiaries of nonprofit services rely on such aid for their particular benefits, but the very character of American life depends on individuals' feelings of mutual obligation and the exercise of pragmatic altruism, which are expressed in and nurtured by private giving for public purposes.

Yet, despite the broadly significant role of private giving, two factors that the Commission has examined cast doubts on whether the level of private giving, in relative and perhaps even absolute terms, is likely to be sustained, let alone increased, without deliberate and energetic efforts toward this end. One factor is the estimation that while the giving of time and labor—volunteer work—has increased in recent years, the giving of money and property has fallen off in relation to the economy as a whole. The other factor is that government's principal encouragement to private giving—the charitable deduction—is being questioned, at least by some, largely in terms of egalitarian values, and is being eroded by other governmental priorities. Neither factor by itself appears to present an immediate severe threat to Americans' deeply ingrained practice of private giving. Yet together, the Commission feels, these are not developments that can or should be ignored.

Thus the first chapter of Part II of this report deals with recommendations involving tax proposals that affect philanthropic giving. This set of recommendations is followed by another which is aimed at improving the "philanthropic process"—the interaction of donor and donee and the public at large that guides giving and nonprofit activity toward socially beneficial purposes—and at building public confidence in the process, which must underlie continuing financial and political support of the nonprofit sector. Finally, this report finds continuous examination, representation and strengthening of the sector to be tasks that call for establishment of a permanent commission on the voluntary sector.

All these recommendations are aimed at sustaining and reinforcing the nonprofit sector as a major institutional area and force in American society. Ultimately, of course, the sector's own performance, the services and functions it provides—or because of institutional inertia and narrow self-interests fails to provide—will do more than any set of structural changes to affect the health and vitality of the sector as a whole.

So an ultimate Commission charge to organizations and institutions of the nonprofit sector is to be constantly aware that though privately controlled, they exist to pursue public purposes and in various ways are answerable to the citizenry as a whole. No institution or set of institutions automatically deserves public support and all must be aware of the need to recurrently demonstrate, by deed and by openness to public examination, their worthiness of this support. At the same time, the Commission cannot stress too much to the American public the importance of sustaining a large and vigorous voluntary sector. While Americans as a whole may take the sector for granted, it is worth noting that most other people in the rest of the world do not. They do not for the simple reason that they have nothing like it. And the Commission feels that they are the poorer for the absence.

VI

BROADENING THE BASE
OF PHILANTHROPY

It is entirely appropriate, this Commission believes, that as a nation we encourage private giving to nonprofit "charitable" organizations and that we do so by governmental means. It is appropriate because these organizations play an indispensable role in American life and because private giving is essential not only to their autonomous existence but also for maintaining the level of services and benefits they provide to ultimate beneficiaries. Governmental encouragements to giving are appropriate, further, because giving provides an important mode of citizen expression. By saying with his or her own·dollars what needs should be met, what objectives pursued, what values served, every contributor exercises, in a profound sense, a form of self-government, a form that parallels, complements and enriches the democratic electoral process itself.*

Yet if the appropriateness of governmental encouragements to giving is, we believe, firmly based and widely accepted, criticisms have arisen in recent years from some quarters concerning the principal existing form of encouragement—the charitable income tax deduction. The main criticism, as noted elsewhere in this report, is that the deduction provides a greater inducement, the higher the giver's income, and that it therefore serves to favor causes of upper-income contributors.

Accordingly, one of the major undertakings of the Commission has been to examine the deduction and possible alternatives to the deduction and to attempt to reach a consensus as to which particular form of encouragement is most suitable to the purposes of charitable giving and the broader purposes of our society.

A number of proposals for new kinds of inducements to giving have been put forward in the last few years; some have

*See comment by MAX M. FISHER, page 201.

123

been developed in detail specifically for the Commission's consideration. In examining and weighing these, along with the existing charitable deduction itself, we have borne in mind a number of objectives—and we have ultimately recognized that no particular form of inducement will fully attain all of these objectives. Indeed, as we have gone through an extensive process of research, analysis and judgment, we have come to realize that there are some virtues and some shortcomings in all of the proposals examined, and that preferences among them must accommodate a variety of often competing considerations.

Objectives

These are the six objectives by which the Commission has weighed different kinds of encouragement to giving:

1. *To increase the number of people who contribute significantly to and participate in nonprofit activities.*

The Commission's survey of taxpayers, described in Chapter II, indicates that giving and direct participation in nonprofit activities—volunteering—tend to go hand in hand. The Commission believes that the number of people who engage in either or both should be increased because of the benefits to society from nonprofit activities, including benefits to the participants in such activities. It is also important for the long-run health and stability of the third sector, the Commission feels, that as many Americans as possible give significant amounts of time and money to, and therefore have a direct interest in the durability of, nonprofit organizations and the nonprofit sector as a whole.

2. *To increase the amount of giving.*

As Chapter II notes, the level of giving by individuals has declined markedly in recent years as a proportion of personal income and of the gross national product. Chapter III describes how giving has declined even more steeply in purchasing power, because goods and services for which contributions are used have gone up in price more than the price level of the economy as a whole. Between declining relative amounts of giving and the exceptionally higher costs facing nonprofit organizations, it is estimated that the relative purchasing power of charitable contributions declined from 2 per cent of GNP in 1960 to 1.5 per cent in 1972. This level has undoubtedly fallen off even further since 1972, as giving itself has decreased, absolutely, in constant dollars.

In order to restore giving to its former level, an increase in contributions of one third would be needed, or around $8 billion based on current giving levels. If such an increase stands as an upper goal for encouragements to giving, a minimum goal is suggested by estimates that giving will have to grow on the average by 11 per cent a year to maintain even its current reduced impact. This estimate is based on projections that the gross national product will grow, in undeflated dollar amounts, by 10 per cent a year for the foreseeable future and on expectations that costs of nonprofit activities will continue to rise 1 per cent faster than costs in general.

A new base level of giving one third higher than at present in order to restore old giving levels and a continuous growth rate of 11 per cent simply to stand still pose no modest range of goals, considering that for the last five years giving has increased only 7 per cent a year on the average, or less than the rate of inflation. Yet the Commission feels that substantial goals must be pursued if an independent third sector is not to slowly erode away or become an adjunct of government because of insufficient private support. Further, even the ambitious goals set forward here relate only to existing or past levels of giving. They may not be ambitious enough, because they do not take into account that many new groups with new purposes and new constituencies have, as observed earlier in this report, sprung up with new demands on the resources of philanthropy. Nor do they take into account ever-growing demands for the services of traditional philanthropic organizations.

3. *To increase the inducement to giving by those in low- and middle-income brackets.*

Within the context of the progressive income tax, the cost of giving a dollar goes down as a contributor's tax bracket goes up. Whether this is inequitable or not can be, and is, argued, and Chapter V summarizes the major sides of the argument. But unquestionably the lower-income giver has less of an inducement to give than does the higher-income donor, and as a practical and political matter, this gives lower-income givers, who constitute a sizable portion of all citizens, less reason to give to and to feel a stake in the nonprofit sector. More than two thirds of all taxpayers, as noted, have no tax inducement to give at all because it is less costly for them to take the standard deduction than it is to take the charitable deduction along with other itemized tax deductions. Thus, apart from considerations of equity, the Commission feels that widely unequal giving inducements create some risk to the continuance of any inducement at all, and to the giving induced. For this reason alone the range in inducements should be narrowed by raising the level of inducements to lower incomes.

4. *To preserve private choice in giving.*

Government currently influences giving through the tax system by determining what is or is not a tax-deductible cause and by setting percentage-of-income deduction limits. For giving to provide a mode of individual expression and of citizen influence on the course of society and its institutions, giving must be contained and influenced as little as possible by collective, governmental determinations or, as one Commission report notes, giving becomes just another way for government to do what it wants to do anyway.

5. *To minimize income losses of nonprofit organizations that depend on the current pattern of giving.*

While the Commission recognizes that the divisions and destinations of the philanthropic dollar have changed considerably over the span of American history, and that they are bound to continue changing as needs change and as priorities of contributors and donees' reliances on public versus private funds themselves shift, the Commission feels that it is not an appropriate time for major decreases in any area of private giving. This is because, as delineated in Chapter III, nearly all nonprofit organizations are facing extreme financial pressures today. Whether, in the long run, inducements to giving should be oriented towards what are today the hardest pressed organizations or whether private giving would better serve public

126

needs if it were guided towards other purposes, is another, broader matter that should be examined by any future study of philanthropy and the nonprofit sector.* For now and the foreseeable future, however, the Commission feels that any inducements to giving should not be constructed so as to discourage giving to current recipients.

6. *To be as "efficient" as possible.*

The new levels of contributions stimulated should at least approximate the amount of government revenue foregone in order to provide this stimulus.

Three Approaches

The Commission has considered, and has weighed in terms of the above objectives, three basic approaches to providing public encouragement to private giving: the charitable deduction itself, including modifications; tax credits; and matching grants. The charitable deduction permits a taxpayer to subtract the amount of his or her giving from the total income upon which taxes are computed. A tax credit permits a taxpayer to subtract a specified amount or percentage of annual giving from the amount of income tax owed. Under matching grant proposals for encouraging giving, the government distributes to charitable organizations a percentage of either the amount each person gives or the amount each organization receives from private sources.

CONTINUING THE DEDUCTION

Members of the Commission are virtually unanimous in concluding that continued use of the charitable deduction should be the primary means of public encouragement of private giving. A number of considerations have led to this conclusion.

*See comment by MAX M. FISHER, page 202.

Giving Should Not Be Taxed

For many Commission members the charitable deduction is a philosophically sound recognition that what a person gives away simply ought not to be considered as income for purposes of imposing an income tax. There is no fixed definition of income; it is a concept that acquires meaning by the context in which the term is used. In the context of personal income taxation, the Commission believes it is appropriate to define income as revenue used for personal consumption or increasing personal wealth and to therefore exclude charitable giving because it is neither. We recognize that in some eyes giving money away can be and is considered a form of consumption. In return for a contribution, a donor in some circumstances may acquire enhanced status in the community, or even power and influence, and will often derive some measure of ego satisfaction.

For countless numbers of donors, however, the Commission believes that private giving is primarily altruistic, that most people do not enhance their wealth or their power when they give and are not providing for their personal needs, and that they should not therefore be taxed on the amount of money they give away. We think it entirely appropriate, in other words, for the person who earns $55,000 and gives $5,000 to charitable organizations to be taxed in exactly the same way as the person who earns $50,000 and gives away nothing.

A Proven Mechanism

The charitable deduction has been a widely accepted device that has been part of the income tax laws virtually since their adoption. It has proven itself simple to administer, requiring little more government manpower or mechanism than is needed in any case for income tax collection and verification. Constitutionally, it stands unassailed, whereas other proposals such as federal matching grants or credit systems risk running afoul of constitutional prohibitions, at least as far as donations to

128

religious organizations are concerned. And it is a familiar device that has come to be relied upon both by those who give and by the institutions to which they give. While these factors alone do not justify retention of the deduction or resistance to departures from the deduction, they do place a burden upon those who criticize the deduction to demonstrate the overall superiority of alternatives.

An "Efficient" Inducement

Commission studies show also that the charitable deduction is a highly "efficient" inducement to giving. Ever since the deduction's enactment six decades ago, an argument has been waged among tax analysts and others interested in the deduction as to whether the amount of tax revenues not collected because of the deduction is matched by at least an equal increase in charitable contributions attributable to the deduction.

When this Commission began its work, there was little hard evidence in answer to this elementary question. What data and analysis there were suggested that tax deductions had only a minor effect on contributions. However, a series of econometric studies on the effectiveness of the deduction undertaken for the Commission by economist Martin Feldstein and colleagues at Harvard University indicates that the increase in charitable contributions induced by the charitable deduction is *greater* than tax revenues lost.

By analyzing, with the aid of computers, aggregate Internal Revenue Service data by income class from 1948 to 1968, household survey data for 1963 compiled by the Federal Reserve Board and Treasury data for 1962 and 1970, Feldstein concluded that for each dollar of tax revenue lost by virtue of the deduction, charitable organizations receive between $1.15 and $1.29 in additional contributions. (In economic terminology, the price elasticities of charitable giving were found to range from -1.15 to -1.29.)

In all, according to projections from these calculations, from $6.7 to $7.5 billion in giving by individuals in fiscal 1976 would be attributable to the loss of $5.8 billion in tax revenues. Feldstein's analysis also indicates that approximately one quarter of all giving is induced by the charitable deduction.

The effectiveness of the charitable deduction was further evidenced, if somewhat equivocally, in the Commission's sample survey of taxpayers. Few taxpayers appeared to know their marginal tax rates and thus few were able to estimate how much lower their net cost of giving was after taking a charitable deduction, and most respondents denied that tax considerations influenced their own charitable giving. Still, those who itemized deductions and thus availed themselves of the charitable deduction reported giving markedly more on the average— at every income level—than those who used the standard deduction. While some of this difference can be accounted for by factors other than use or nonuse of the charitable deduction, a conclusion of the survey was that the differences "are so large as to imply there must be a substantial tax incentive to charity" among itemizers. The differences are shown in the table on the following page.

Insulation from Government

Another major virtue of the deduction is its relative insulation from political or bureaucratic manipulation. Compared with other forms of encouragement such as matching grants, the deduction as a mechanism is not subject to fine-tuning to fit administratively or legislatively determined goals. It thus leaves the greatest leeway to individual, as contrasted to collective, determination of giving patterns, and this is seen as being of decisive importance in maintaining the pluralistic role that the nonprofit sector should play. Congress and the Internal Revenue Service, to be sure, exercise definite limitations on the charitable deduction through their respective powers to decide and to interpret decisions as to which organizations may receive tax-deductible gifts. And in recent years, some groups have complained that the IRS has used its power improperly to disqualify certain organizations for narrow political or ideological reasons. Yet the power to determine donee eligibility

AVERAGE GIVING BY INCOME OF ITEMIZERS

AND NON-ITEMIZERS

1973

Adjusted Gross Income	Itemized	Did Not Itemize
Less than $4,000	$ 119*	$ 69
$4,000 – 7,999	215	89
$8,000 – 9,999	314	117
$10,000 – 14,999	407	201
$15,000 – 19,999	600	329
$20,000 – 29,999	800	354
$30,000 – 49,999	1,564	171*
$50,000 – 99,999	5,679	3,190*
$100,000 – 199,999	17,106	816*
$200,000 – 499,999	39,763	8,892*
$500,000 or more	71,316	5,000*

*Based on fewer than 25 observations

Source: Sample survey for the Commission on Private Philanthropy and Public
Needs by the Survey Research Center of the Institute for Social Research
at the University of Michigan and the U.S. Census Bureau

would presumably have to accompany any other form of government encouragement to giving while in addition other proposed forms, because of easier adjustability of their mechanisms, would offer opportunities for recurrent governmental review and manipulation.

Matching grants and credits are also, the Commission feels, more susceptible to political manipulation because they can be seen to involve government funds. Matching grants in fact would flow directly from the Treasury. And the government can reasonably be considered to have an equally strong claim to funds involved in tax credits, because such funds would otherwise have to be paid in taxes. The Commission recognizes that there are those who consider money given to charity to be government money as well if it is deducted from income on which taxes are based, but the Commission emphatically does not share this view. We understand, of course, that the federal government now computes a tax-expenditure budget and includes in that calculation the amount of taxes not collected because of the charitable deduction. We have no quarrel with that inclusion as a bookkeeping technique. But it does not transform a private gift into a government grant, nor should it subject deductible giving to the same potential for manipulation that the Commission feels hovers over matching grants and tax credits as true users of government funds.

Allocation Effects

In favoring retention of the charitable deduction, the Commission was also concerned about the different allocation of philanthropic giving that elimination of or substitution for the deduction would, the evidence indicates, effect. As Chapter II of this report observes, the destination as well as the amount of giving differs markedly among income levels. Add to this the fact that the current tax deduction system makes the cost of giving lower, the higher a giver's income and that a lower cost appears to be a highly effective inducement to giving. What follows is that current giving patterns under the deduction reflect the preferences of upper incomes quite out of proportion to their numbers alone.* It also follows that any significant leveling down of current giving inducements would reduce giving to the types of recipients generally chosen by upper-income givers. Feldstein's studies include the following projection, based on 1970 income and tax figures, of what would happen if the charitable deduction were totally eliminated:

Taxpayers having incomes of $10,000 to $15,000 would reduce their gifts by 22 per cent (from an average of $290 to $225). Taxpayers in the $100,000 to $500,000 class would cut back their giving by 75 per cent, from average annual contributions of $9,184 to $2,246. In all, the total of $17.3 billion in individual giving estimated for 1970 would be reduced by 26 per cent if there were no deduction. What would the effect on recipients be? Giving to religious organizations, where contributions by lower-income Americans predominantly go, would fall by 22 per cent. Gifts to educational institutions and hospitals, to which higher-income givers direct a large share of their contributions, would drop by nearly one half.

The effect of simply eliminating the deduction would, in other words, bear heavily on current recipients of philanthropy, particularly traditional secular institutions that are, as Chapter III describes, among the financially hardest pressed of nonprofit organizations.

The effect of replacing the deduction with a tax credit or a matching grant would be similar, to the extent that any such alternatives cut down inducements to higher-income givers and increased them for lower. Thus a 30 per cent charitable tax credit, which was one of the proposals the Commission considered, would induce approximately 9 per cent more giving than the current deduction does, according to the Commission's econometric projections. But because a 30 per cent credit provides more of a tax saving than most low- and middle-income taxpayers now enjoy using a deduction and less than most high-income taxpayers enjoy, giving to education and to hospitals would decrease by around one third each, while giving to religion would rise by around 14 per cent, absorbing most of the overall increase in contributions.

*See comment by MAX M. FISHER, page 203.

Reflecting the Progressive Income Tax

In expressing a strong preference for the charitable deduction as the basic governmental incentive for private giving, the Commission recognizes that this approach is subject to criticism on the ground that it creates an inverse relationship between the cost of giving and an individual's income tax bracket. The net cost after taxes of giving one dollar is 86 cents for someone in the 14 per cent bracket and only 30 cents for someone in the 70 per cent bracket. Plainly the charitable deduction makes giving less costly for those in the higher tax brackets. It must also be recognized, however, that this result is a consequence of the progressive rate structure of the income tax. The upper-income taxpayer pays not only more tax dollars than the lower-income taxpayer but also pays taxes at a higher rate.

Since most members of the Commission believe it is philosophically sound not to consider money given to charity as income, they accept the consequences that a progressive rate structure applies to the relative costs of giving.

"Leadership Effect"

Further, while it is recognized that the present deduction does give more inducement to someone in a higher income bracket than someone in a lower bracket, it is also recognized that, as a practical matter, the giving of large sums by those in higher brackets often leads others to give and that this "leadership effect" can be a significant element in spurring giving as a whole.

EXTENDING AND AMPLIFYING
THE DEDUCTION

On balance, the Commission believes that the virtues of the charitable deduction significantly outweigh its defects as both virtues and defects have evidenced themselves over six decades of the deduction's existence. We are also strongly persuaded that in comparison with other inducements to giving, the charitable deduction is preferable and should remain as the basic governmental encouragement of private giving. The Commission recognizes, however, that some changes are required both to broaden the base of private giving and to meet some of the criticism that the charitable deduction has encountered. We therefore recommend:

1. *That to increase inducements for charitable giving, all taxpayers who take the standard deduction should also be permitted to deduct charitable contributions as an additional, itemized deduction.*

2. *That an additional inducement to charitable giving should be provided to low- and middle-income taxpayers. Toward this end, the Commission proposes that a "double deduction" be instituted for families with incomes of less than $15,000 a year; they would be allowed to deduct twice what they give in computing their income taxes. For those families with incomes between $15,000 and $30,000, the Commission proposes a deduction of 150 per cent of their giving.**

Extending the Charitable Deduction

In recent years, as noted earlier in this report, a significant development has occurred with respect to the income tax laws that has made the charitable deduction less of an inducement to low- and middle-income taxpayers. This development is the rising level of the "standard deduction"—the sum of money that the tax laws allow each taxpayer to deduct in lieu of all

*See dissents by ELIZABETH J. McCORMACK, page 203, by GRACIELA OLIVAREZ, page 204, and by ALAN PIFER, page 205.

the itemized deductions to which he or she is entitled. For married taxpayers filing joint returns, the maximum standard deduction has risen from $1,000 in 1970 to $2,600 in 1975. This increase in the standard deduction has brought about a marked decrease in the proportion of taxpayers who itemize their deductions and who thus derive any benefit at all from the charitable deduction. In 1970, nearly one half of taxpayers used the charitable deduction; now fewer than one third do. The falloff of those taking the charitable deduction coincides with and may partly account for the relative sluggishness of overall charitable giving in recent years.

Extending the deduction would make it available to the nearly 60 million taxpayers who do not currently benefit from it as an inducement to giving because they take the standard deduction. According to Feldstein's econometric projections made for the Commission, giving would increase by $1.9 billion in 1976, or an average of about $40 per taxpayer newly reached by the charitable deduction. The reduction in government tax revenues because of increased use of the deduction would be around $1.7 billion.

This increase in giving and decrease in tax revenues would result because extending the deduction would give nearly 60 million taxpayers in effect at least a 14 per cent tax writeoff on every charitable dollar, where they now face no tax saving directly attributable to giving. The 14 per cent figure represents the minimum income-tax bracket, in which deducting a dollar of charitable giving has the effect of lowering taxes by 14 cents. Taxpayers in higher brackets would enjoy a correspondingly higher tax-savings and receive a correspondingly greater inducement to give.

The Commission believes that extending the deduction to non-itemizers would go a long way toward meeting several of the objectives the Commission has set down. Both the number of those giving significant amounts of time and/or money and the overall level of giving should increase sizably. Nine tenths of taxpayers with incomes above $25,000 itemize their deductions. Therefore recipient areas favored by lower income levels would receive most of the increased giving, but not at the expense of other areas. Extending the deduction, moreover,

136

would maintain a principal virtue of the deduction itself—its relative insulation from government manipulation.

We recognize, of course, that the proponents of every deduction presently allowed by the tax laws could argue with equal plausibility that the use of each deduction would be increased if it were available as an itemized deduction in addition to the standard deduction. If all such arguments prevailed, there would be no point in having a standard deduction, which was introduced into the tax laws to serve the important purpose of promoting simplification in filling out tax forms. The case for allowing the charitable deduction to be itemized by those using the standard deduction rests, however, on the proposition that the charitable deduction is in a real sense different from all other deductions and entitled to special, preferential treatment.

The difference lies in underlying rationales for tax deductions. The two most common are: to alleviate the impact of extraordinary, unanticipated expenses and to encourage a particular type of expenditure. Among deductions enacted for the first reason are those for higher than normal medical expenses. Among the latter are deductions for interest on home mortgages, designed to promote home ownership. Both types of deductions involve expenditures to satisfy personal needs.

By contrast, the charitable deduction provides an incentive for an expenditure whose essential characteristic is promotion of public purposes. And significantly, unlike the payment of state taxes, which is also deductible and which also supports public purposes, the charitable expenditure is entirely volitional. It is the only expenditure for public purposes that each person decides individually whether or not to make. We do not doubt the hardship of excessive medical expenses nor the virtues of home ownership. We do contend that private giving is essential to the nature and quality of life in American society. Because of the fundamental importance of the dollars spent and the urgent need to increase the number of donors and the number of dollars they give, the principal governmental incentive to private giving should be recognized as a special deduction, broadly available to all taxpayers, whether or not they use the standard deduction.

137

Extending the charitable deduction to those who presently do not itemize will regrettably detract somewhat from simplified preparation of tax returns. The taxpayer now using the standard deduction can determine from a table what taxes are owed, or, if the taxpayer's income is $20,000 or less, the IRS itself will calculate the tax bill. If the charitable deduction were available outside the standard deduction, any taxpayer using it would have to subtract charitable giving (plus the standard deduction and personal and dependent exemptions) from his or her income, and then compute the tax. Of course, no taxpayer would be required to do so; use of the charitable deduction would simply be available in addition to the standard deduction for every taxpayer who was willing to put up with the slight extra inconvenience. We think that many of the nearly 60 million taxpayers who now take the standard deduction would be willing to avail themselves of an additional, itemized charitable deduction and that donee organizations would explain the virtues of doing so. The added inconvenience, we believe, is far outweighed by the additional private giving to be generated and, perhaps of greater importance, the enlistment of millions of people into a new pattern of private giving.

A New Incentive for Low- and Middle-Income Contributors

While extending the charitable deduction to nonitemizers would provide an inducement for giving to millions of taxpayers who now derive no tax savings in connection with their contributions, the Commission recognizes that at the lowest income levels, the inducement would still be small in comparison to that available to highest-income contributors—14 cents in tax savings for each dollar given as against 70 cents.

Moreover, the amount of giving that can be induced by the regular charitable deduction is strictly limited, and the $1.9 billion increase that is projected for extending the reach of the deduction to all taxpayers falls considerably short of the $8 billion goal needed to restore giving to its former relative level. Therefore, the Commission has considered a variety of additional proposals to stimulate giving further and to provide low- and middle-income contributors in particular an additional incentive for giving.

A minority of the Commission members favored some form of tax credit for providing this additional inducement.* But the majority preferred to stay within the deduction mechanism. Very little support was expressed for government matching grants as a way of further stimulating giving. These are some of the proposals and considerations that were involved in the Commission reckonings.

A Supplementary Credit

Commission members favoring tax credits tended to be persuaded in this direction mainly by the fact that, unlike the deduction, credits operate independently of the progressive structure of the income tax and therefore provide the same proportionate tax savings to all taxpayers regardless of their income. Under a 25 per cent credit, for instance, every taxpayer could subtract 25 per cent of his contributions from the taxes he or she owes. This uniformity of inducement was seen by some Commission members as being more equitable than the deduction and was considered preferable for this reason.

Perhaps the most dramatic credit proposal that the Commission considered was to allow every taxpayer a 100 per cent credit up to $100 of charitable giving. Every taxpayer could thereby reduce his or her taxes by $100 by giving $100 to charity. Every donee organization could solicit $100 contributions from every taxpayer, using the seemingly irresistible argument that the donation would literally not cost a penny. Unfortunately, according to the Commission's econometric projections, a credit designed in this fashion would stimulate very little new giving; these projections suggest that its principal effect would be a reduction in taxes by those who now give. The 100 per cent-$100 credit, it is estimated, would generate $500 million in new giving at a revenue loss of $5 billion.

Some Commission members questioned the assumptions

*See comment by ELIZABETH J. McCORMACK, page 205.

upon which these projections were based, feeling that they do not take into account a new dynamic that would be set in motion by the $100 credit. And the Commission as a whole realizes of course that such projections must be weighed with caution, based as they are on certain simplified models of human motivations and behavior in an area in which motivations and behavior are anything but simple. Yet even granting the uncertainties surrounding projections of the impact of new giving incentives, few members of the Commission were willing to endorse a technique that might operate anywhere near as inefficiently as the projections indicate—producing only one dollar of increased giving for every ten in tax revenues uncollected.

Far more "efficient," according to the projections, would be partial tax credits, by which taxpayers could credit a portion, say 25 or 30 per cent, of giving against the taxes they owe. In general, such partial credits are projected as increasing giving more than they decrease tax revenues.

The Commission considered both optional and "add-on" partial credits. Under an optional credit, all taxpayers would have the choice of either using the credit or using the deduction to reduce their taxes in connection with charitable giving, whichever provided the largest reduction. The add-on credit the Commission considered would be allowed to taxpayers, below a specified income ceiling, as an addition to the deduction. Contributors would be able first to deduct their giving from income in calculating their taxes, and then to subtract a percentage of the same giving—10 per cent in the specific formula the Commission considered—from the tax obligation itself.

Even as supplements to, rather than substitutes for, the deduction, however, tax credits for giving were regarded with some skepticism by most Commission members because any charitable tax credit was seen as a potential step toward substituting a credit for the charitable deduction altogether.*

*See comment by MAX M. FISHER, page 207.

The Double Deduction

Instead, a majority preferred a new, extra deduction as a means of providing further inducements to low- and middle-income givers and of increasing the level of giving. The formula favored was a 200 per cent "double" deduction for families with incomes of under $15,000 (or for individuals with incomes below $7,500) and a 150 per cent deduction for families with incomes between $15,000 and $30,000 (individuals between $7,500 and $15,000). The Commission recognized that in the drafting of legislation this proposal would have to be technically refined.

This addition to the Commission's recommended extension of the charitable deduction to non-itemizers would have the effect of doubling the potential tax savings for giving for all taxpayers whose income falls below $15,000 and of raising the savings by one half for those in the $15,000-to-$30,000 income range. The current minimum tax savings for itemizers—14 cents on the contributed dollar, corresponding to the minimum 14 per cent tax bracket—would rise to 28 cents on the dollar. Tax savings for those with higher marginal tax rates would rise accordingly—up to around 48 cents on the dollar for a family of four close to the $30,000 income limit, whose marginal tax rate averages around 32 per cent.

Not only would the extra deduction provide a substantial additional inducement for giving to low- and middle-income taxpayers, but according to projections both the amount of giving induced and the "efficiency" of inducing it would be impressive. The extra deduction would increase giving by as much as $9.8 billion, at a tax loss of $7.4 billion. When these amounts are added to changes from extending the deduction to non-itemizers, the overall increase in giving from both extending and amplifying the deduction is projected to be $11.7 billion, with a corresponding $9.1 billion decrease in tax revenues.

Use of an extra deduction as an incentive was preferred by most Commission members for all of the reasons that make the charitable deduction itself the basic preferred means of stimulating private giving. In addition to those virtues, an extra

141

deduction is seen as having the special advantage of being easily understood. An inducement to giving directed especially at those in low- and middle-income brackets, who infrequently receive guidance from tax experts, should be clearly and readily understandable to be effective, and many members felt that people would readily understand and respond to a tax provision that permits deduction of twice or one and a half times the level of contributions.

While recommending this extra deduction as the best means for broadening the base of charitable giving, the Commission recognizes that other considerations such as the budgetary impact of the extra deduction must be considered by Congress in determining how and when such a proposal can be implemented. It should be borne in mind in any such consideration, however, that the net budgetary impact would be less than the tax loss projected since the charitable contributions stimulated would to some extent reduce the need for governmental expenditures in the areas to which the new giving would go. The Commission is also aware of the administrative concerns which must be taken into account in implementing these deduction proposals. We would anticipate, for example, that the IRS would make appropriate requirements, such as written proof of contributions, in order to assure protection of tax revenues.

In addition to our consideration of basic incentives for charitable giving and specific techniques for increasing contributions by all individuals and providing an increased incentive for giving by low- and middle-income groups, the Commission has also focused upon several specific issues that arise in connection with charitable giving and tax policy. These concern the minimum tax, gifts of appreciated property, charitable bequests and corporate giving.

MINIMUM TAX

Lying just beneath the surface of any consideration of philanthropy and taxes is the view held by some that charitable deductions, particularly for those in higher-income brackets, are "loopholes," just another way to avoid paying their fair share of taxes. One response to this viewpoint has been efforts to include under any new minimum income tax legislation the amount of income a person gives to charity. The effect of such an inclusion would be, in some circumstances, to make a person's charitable contributions subject to tax, and to therefore lower the overall level of giving.

A minimum tax device is now contained in the Internal Revenue Code. It does not cover charitable deductions. But there has been considerable debate in Congress and in the Administration in recent years, particularly among tax experts, as to whether any new minimum tax legislation should include the charitable deduction. Those who advocate inclusion say that without it, some taxpayers would still be able to pay little or no income tax. Others do not accept this argument. The Treasury Department, which had previously supported including the deduction, reversed itself in mid-1975 and advocated exclusion—"in view of the dire financial position in which inflation has left so many private charities."

This Commission does not consider deductible charitable giving to constitute a tax loophole, and it does not consider the time and economic circumstances as appropriate, in any case, for any measure that would have the effect of reducing giving. Therefore, the Commission recommends:

*That income deducted for charitable giving should be excluded from any minimum tax provision.**

APPRECIATED PROPERTY**

Soon after the charitable deduction became part of the federal tax law covering the income tax, in 1917, the Internal Revenue Service was called upon to make what seemed to be an innocuous and not widely significant ruling. When property—in the form of stock or a work of art, for instance—was given to charity, how was that property to be valued as a

*See dissent by ELIZABETH J. McCORMACK, page 207.
**See comment by MAX M. FISHER, page 208.

143

deduction from taxable income? The IRS decided that the current market value of the property should be deductible rather than simply the cost to the giver.

But if the implications of the decision seemed slight at the time, in recent decades the tax treatment of "appreciated property" gifts to charity has come under strong attack from certain sources. It is perhaps the most controversial issue which the Commission has considered. The controversy stems from the fact that the appreciated property ruling provides an added inducement for property contributions—so much of an inducement that a contributor stands to benefit financially in extreme cases by giving away property rather than selling it—and this inducement is one that applies almost exclusively to very high-income donors.

Based on estimates prepared by the Treasury, approximately 50 per cent of reported property gifts are made by persons having annual incomes of $100,000 or more. Polling for the Commission by the University of Michigan's Survey Research Center (see page 55) found that only a small percentage of people in the lower-income categories made non-money gifts to charity, but the percentage rises at the highest incomes, reaching 47 per cent for those with incomes of $500,000 or more and accounting for 80 per cent of all charitable giving by this group. Thus the appreciated property provision is a principal target of those who claim that the income tax deduction for charity inequitably amplifies the influence of wealth within the charitable sector.

The appreciated property deduction acts as a strong inducement to giving by taxpayers interested in selling rather than holding on to property, because of its relation to other tax laws, particularly the tax on capital gains. By giving property to charity instead of selling it, the giver does not have to pay a capital gains tax on the appreciated value of the property, and this means that the tax savings from a gift may be close to or even in some cases exceed the proceeds after taxes if the property is sold.

The appreciated property tax allowances provide added inducements to give that are not related to the value of the gift to the charitable recipient. Two people with the same income

144

and giving the same amount to charity are treated differently, depending upon whether one gives cash and the other property. Further, since the after-tax cost of the contribution is related to the increase in value of the donated property, the size of tax inducement does not correspond to the size of the benefit obtained by the charitable recipient or society as a whole. In short, the critics argue that the treatment of appreciated property cannot be justified on principle.

This is, in essence, the case against the appreciated property allowance, and it is a case that has been energetically made by tax reform advocates in recent years. Proponents of the existing tax allowance for appreciated property make several counter-points, however.

First, many institutions rely heavily for support on appreciated property gifts, primarily private colleges, universities, hospitals and cultural organizations that tend to be the principal recipients of contributions by upper-income givers. This is not only because proportionately more high-income givers give non-cash gifts than do lower-income donors. It is also because at upper-income levels those who give appreciated property give far more generously than those who contribute only cash. Treasury statistics show that the average gift by non-cash givers with incomes of $500,000 or more is four times the size of the average gift of those at the same income level who give only in cash. Thus, according to computerized simulations, overall giving would drop by 3 per cent if the appreciated property allowance were eliminated, and the greatest proportion of the loss would be borne by educational organizations, which could expect an 8 per cent decrease in private funds they receive, or around $50 million less a year, based on 1970 dollar values. Many institutions assert that support induced by the appreciated property allowance is critical to the sustaining of their customary standards, some to their very existence.

In addition, proponents of the appreciated property provision point out that the cases where the donor actually benefits from giving are exceedingly rare. Moreover, they argue that any "tax savings" from exclusions of appreciated property from capital gains tax is illusory since the donor is not compelled to either sell or donate property; the donor may retain the property until death and thereby, under current tax laws, avoid capital gains tax liability entirely; imposing a tax upon lifetime property donations, according to this argument, would dry up or defer gifts to charitable organizations.*

Perhaps the most compelling argument heard by the Commission in favor of retaining the appreciated property deduction follows from the last observation—the point being that the appreciated property provision cannot be looked at, legally or socially, in isolation. The fact is that property can now pass, with its appreciated value untaxed, to heirs at death or to others in non-charitable gifts during life. As long as these provisions are part of the tax law, the Commission feels it makes little sense to tax such appreciation only when a gift goes to a charitable organization. Such a limited change in the taxation of appreciated property would simply reduce gifts to charity with only slight increase in revenue to the Treasury. Most of those now giving appreciated property to charity would not continue their giving pattern and pay tax on the value of the appreciation. They would stop making such charitable gifts and transfer the property instead to family and friends during life or hold it for similar disposition at death.

Recommendation

While many Commission members agree that the appreciated property provision in the charitable deduction, when looked at by itself, challenges standards of both tax principle and social equity, it is also felt that the provision must be looked at in a broad context and that when it is, its positive features outweigh its negative ones. Part of that context includes the good that is derived from gifts of appreciated property. Another part is the general tax milieu in which the appreciated property provision exists and from which it cannot be analytically separated. Accordingly, the Commission feels that the appreciated property provision should be retained. At the same time, it feels that clearly no one should be able to actually realize a net financial gain through use of the charitable de-

*See comment by BAYARD EWING, page 209.

146

duction. The Commission therefore recommends:

That the appreciated property allowance within the charitable deduction be basically retained but amended to eliminate any possibility of personal financial gain through tax-deductible charitable giving.*

CHARITABLE BEQUESTS

". . .A hand in the contribution boxes of the country." In 1902 the House Ways and Means Committee so described an 1894 federal inheritance tax law which did not except from taxation bequests to charitable organizations. The federal estate tax law, its modern descendant, permits a deduction for charitable bequests, a deduction that has inspired nearly as much controversy in recent years as its counterpart in the income tax.

Bequests are an important source of voluntary support for private nonprofit organizations. According to *Giving USA*, charitable gifts at death of $2.07 billion accounted for 10 per cent of total giving by individuals to charity in 1974. Between 1965 and 1974, charitable bequests more than doubled, from less than $1.02 billion to more than $2.07 billion. In 1970-1971, transfers at death furnished almost 17 per cent of voluntary support to the 1,080 private colleges and universities surveyed by the American Council on Education.

Substantial charitable bequests were made before the advent of the modern estate tax. But since their enactment in 1916, federal death taxes have been a major stimulant for private giving. The federal estate tax is imposed on all property owned or controlled by a person at death, with offsets allowed for expenses, debts, taxes, charitable bequests and bequests to one's spouse (limited to 50 per cent of the estate), and a $60,000 exemption. The tax affects only a small, the wealthiest, segment of the population. About 9 per cent of all adult decedents own more than $60,000 at death, requiring the filing of some 175,000 estate tax returns in 1973. Of these returns, only 121,000 were taxable, meaning that 6 per cent of all estates

*See comment by GRACIELA OLIVAREZ, page 209.

were liable for any estate tax. Treasury Department correlations of income and wealth indicate that estate tax is paid almost exclusively by families with incomes above $20,000.

Within this segment of society, the steeply progressive rates of the estate tax, rising to 77 per cent on taxable transfers in excess of $10 million, do affect how property is passed at death. A wealthy person is given few choices in disposing of his or her property. The incentive to leave funds to charity is strong: in estates which exceed $5 million, $125 went to charity for every $100 bequeathed to individuals.

Tax inducements to charitable bequests have been subject to some of the same criticisms and proposals for changes as has the charitable income tax deduction, and in considering possible alternatives to the current system for bequests, the Commission has looked at them in terms of many of the same criteria it applied to the income tax deduction and alternatives to that measure.

Equity

Because the choice for wealthy individuals is largely between leaving their property to charity or paying it to the government as taxes, the charitable bequest deduction can be characterized as enabling these individuals "to make decisions concerning the expenditure of public revenue, or, somewhat more accurately," writes Richard E. Wagner, of Virginia Polytechnic Institute, "the expenditure of what otherwise would have been public revenue." Such decisions are limited to those of that narrow segment of society that pays estate tax, and the power is allocated within this group in relation to their wealth and the tax rates imposed on their estates. The wealthiest 2 per cent of taxable decedents' estates (or less than two tenths of 1 per cent of all decedents' estates) account for 63 per cent of all deductions for charitable bequests.

So the main benefit of tax deductions for such bequests goes to organizations selected by wealthy benefactors. And not surprisingly, critics indict the bequest deduction for allowing wealthy testators to exert what they believe to be a disproportionately large influence on the use of what would otherwise be government revenues. As in the case of the income tax deduction, matching grants and credits have been proposed as an alternative to the bequest deduction.

There is, however, another view of the federal estate tax which fully justifies the equity of the bequest deduction, rendering resort to matching grants or tax credits unnecessary if not unwise. President Franklin Roosevelt in 1935 urged a sharp increase in estate tax rates to near their present levels in order to prevent the concentration of static wealth in private hands. "Great accumulations of wealth," he said "cannot be justified on the basis of personal and family security." Indeed, both Theodore Roosevelt and Andrew Carnegie considered that the principal virtue of heavy death taxation was its limitation on the transfer of excessive accumulations of wealth.

If the main purpose of the estate tax is regarded as a limitation on the passing of wealth to private hands in the next generation, then charitable bequests should not be taxed. Transfers to charitable organizations are consistent with the purposes of the estate tax since they remove wealth from direct private control and commit it to what are deemed to be public purposes. As Martin Feldstein points out, because the deduction is an effective incentive for charitable bequests, "private intergenerational transfers of wealth to individuals are therefore reduced [and] because charitable gifts are increased by more than taxes are reduced, the personal heirs now receive less than they would if the current deductions were eliminated." Taxing charitable bequests or otherwise discouraging them would defeat a principal objective of the estate tax.

Allocation Effects

Whatever the equities, switching to matching grants or tax credits may not be sound as a matter of public policy because of the effect that change might have on organizations which receive a major share of tax-induced bequests. Hard information is lacking, but one study suggests that social welfare organizations received 45 per cent of estimated charitable bequests reported in estate tax returns filed in 1957 and 1959; scientific, literary, and educational organizations received 23 per cent of

149

these bequests; religion, 14 per cent; and all other organizations (which includes foundations), 17 per cent.

Again, Feldstein determined that the percentage of estates bequeathed to religious organizations remains fairly constant for estates of all sizes, but the percentage given to private educational organizations tends to increase as the size of the estate increases. This implies that bequests to private educational organizations are more sensitive to the tax inducement than bequests to religion. Any change in the tax law that reduces the bequest incentive can be expected to affect private colleges and universities more severely than churches.

Using different data sources, Michael J. Boskin, a Stanford economist, comes to the same general conclusion. He estimates from 1969 data that if the deduction were replaced by a 30 per cent estate tax credit, the Treasury would gain about $227 million in taxes, but charitable organizations would lose bequests totalling $360 million. Because educational and social welfare organizations tend to receive bequests from testators at the upper end of the estate tax rate structure, a reduction in the tax incentive would result in their loss of $353 million, while churches would lose only $7 million.

Percentage Limits

Even if the deduction is retained, others urge that it should be limited. Unlike income tax charitable deductions, which are restricted to 50 per cent of income, there is no percentage limit on bequest deductions. This means that a testator can choose not to pay estate tax by bequeathing all his property to charity. Evoking a sentiment which underlies the minimum income tax idea, critics assert that no tax should be avoidable as a matter of personal option, that all estates, therefore, even those bequeathed entirely to charity should pay some death tax. A 50 per cent limit on the amount of an estate that could be deducted for charitable giving is one of the main proposals put forward to assure that some estate tax is paid.

However, Boskin's analysis suggests that there would be questionable benefits at best in restricting the bequest deduction to a 50 per cent ceiling. While only 2 per cent of estates filing estate tax returns give more than 50 per cent to charity, the amount given is substantial—$338 million in 1969 dollars, or about one sixth of all charitable bequests. Limiting the deduction to 50 per cent would cause about half these bequests not to be made. Boskin estimates that charitable organizations would lose $189 million in bequests, while estate tax revenues would increase by $43 million, a loss of $4.40 to charity for each dollar gained by the Treasury. In other words, a 50 per cent ceiling on charitable bequests would appear to substantially reduce the flow of funds to nonprofit organizations.

Recommendation

The Commission was not persuaded that any of the suggested changes in the charitable bequest deduction would make the system more equitable. Instead, the changes would reduce bequests to private organizations, particularly to private colleges and universities, without much being gained in equity or tax revenues. Therefore, the Commission recommends:

*That the charitable bequest deduction be retained in its present form.**

CORPORATE GIVING

Near the depths of the Great Depression, in 1935, Congress amended the Internal Revenue Code to allow corporations to deduct charitable contributions from their taxable income. In doing so, Congress in effect gave national approval and encouragement to the practice of giving by corporations to nonprofit activities, a practice that had been growing, slowly, since pre-Civil War days when railroads contributed to the construction of YMCA buildings around the country, and more rapidly since World War I when corporations contributed heavily to local War Chests and to Red Cross campaigns.

At the same time that it allowed charitable deductions for contributions, Congress put a 5 per cent limit on the propor-

*See dissent by GRACIELA OLIVAREZ, page 210.

tion of net income that any corporation could deduct. This limit reflected the viewpoint that had been expressed in earlier court decisions barring charitable contributions by corporations—the view that the business of business is business and that a company had an obligation to confine the use of its resources directly to the pursuit of profit, an obligation both to its shareholders and to the society at large, which according to classical economic analysis was served best when producers of goods or services attempted to maximize profits.

Reservations about corporate giving to charitable activity are still expressed in these terms by some economic conservatives. Ironically, in their doubts about or outright opposition to corporate giving, conservative skeptics are joined from the opposite end of the political spectrum by those who regard corporate giving as an instrument of corporate conservatism. ". . .It is especially inapposite for business corporations to play any role in the philanthropic process," asserts an activist critique addressed to the Commission, a critique that advocates redistribution of wealth as the principal role of giving and nonprofit activity. ". . .The real problem posed by corporate 'philanthropic' activity is that corporations are the embodiment of concentrated wealth. As such, they can hardly be expected to underwrite the political needs of Americans who wish to redistribute and deconcentrate that wealth."

Still, corporate giving has tended to be more and more accepted, and indeed relied upon, by the philanthropic world in the positive light that underlay the granting of tax deductions for such giving, and the 5 per cent limit accordingly has tended to be regarded less as a restraint than a hopeful goal.

Changes in attitudes and philosophies about the relationship of business and society account for changing attitudes about corporate philanthropy. Corporations increasingly have been regarded as having obligations that transcend profit-making; the market place is no longer generally seen as the only appropriate dictator of corporate behavior. Related to a broadened public perception of the social role of corporations is a widening sense by corporations themselves of their own institutional self-interests. In the sights of many modern corporate managers and owners, profit-making is accompanied by—some analysts

152

have even found it to be secondary to—long-term institutional survival and growth.

The influence of such viewpoints on giving is reflected in a survey of some 400 corporate chairmen and presidents made for the Commission by The Conference Board. The corporate leaders were asked to indicate the most important reasons for making contributions. The reasons that were most frequently cited were "corporate citizenship" and "protecting and improving the business environment." (Altruism, by comparison, was mentioned by few executives.) "A company . . . simply cannot sit back with an outmoded concept that its only objective is profitability," said one executive in the survey in explaining why he felt a company should have a contributions and public service program. "The corporation operates as part of a greater society," said another executive. ". . .It takes a healthy society for corporations to operate; they should contribute to that health."

As the idea has grown that corporate giving is both an obligation and a matter of institutional self-interest, so have both the amount and the relative level of corporate giving. Until the Second World War, giving had generally averaged less than one half of 1 per cent of the net income of corporations. By the late 1950's the proportion had doubled. Moreover, this increase only takes account of giving deducted on corporate tax returns; it does not include giving that is counted as a business expense nor does it include non-cash aid and other forms of socially beneficial activities that have also increased under the banner of "corporate social responsibility." These additional "contributions," in the broad sense of the word, include: investments—in areas such as urban renewal and environmental preservation—that corporations would ordinarily not make because of the risk involved; job training for the disadvantaged and for the physically and mentally handicapped; "loans" of employees, on company time and company payrolls, to give technical assistance to charitable organizations and to government. According to a Conference Board estimate, if a price tag were put on such activities, corporate giving of around $1 billion in 1974 would be at least doubled.

The Commission recognizes, moreover, that the primary, if

153

not only, business of business is still business and that a corporation's benefits to society stem mainly from how it conducts its basic operations, from its relations to its customers, its employees, its owners and the public. In any particular corporation's overall role as a responsible social institution, in other words, giving is bound to play a relatively small and limited part.

At the same time, the profit sector's support has come to be an important element in several parts of the nonprofit sector, and the Commission believes that such support can and should be a considerably larger factor in the future—that, indeed, corporate giving remains the last major undeveloped frontier for private giving to philanthropic causes.

Corporate giving can be larger, the Commission believes, in light of the vast funds that flow through corporate treasuries, and it should be larger, both as an exercise of the corporate world's social responsibilities and, ultimately, because of this world's own self-interest in preserving a strong and healthy nonprofit sector as a balance to government.

The Commission's belief that corporate giving can and should be larger reflects the fact that while corporate giving has grown over the long range it has stood still as a proportion of corporate income in recent years, at around 1 per cent of net income. In fact, the evidence is that most companies still do little or no giving at all. Of some 1.7 million corporations that filed income tax returns in 1970, only 20 per cent reported any charitable contributions and only 6 per cent made contributions of over $500. The bulk of giving comes from a comparative handful of corporations, the largest ones; nearly 50 per cent of contributions come from fewer than 1,000 companies.

In line with the Commission's examination of means to encourage greater giving by individuals, the Commission has studied proposed tax law changes aimed at stimulating corporate giving as well. Among them:

—A "disappearing floor" that would permit corporations to take a charitable deduction only when corporate contributions are at or above a given percentage of net income before taxes. Possibilities include a floor of 1 per cent or 2 per cent.

—A 10 per cent tax credit that would permit the corpora-

154

tion, if its contributions exceeded the floor, to take credit for 10 per cent of its charitable giving in the computation of its federal income tax. This credit would be in addition to the deduction.

—A 10 per cent tax credit in addition to the deduction and without a floor. That is, the 10 per cent credit would simply be added to the current deduction available for any corporate giving from zero up to the limit of 5 per cent of net income before taxes.

—A 2 per cent "philanthropic needs" tax, which would be added on to the basic corporate income tax. Any corporation would have the option of fulfilling this tax obligation either by dispensing the amount of the tax to tax-deductible causes or by paying it to the government as it would a regular tax.

The Commission's analysis of these alternatives involved consideration of the following:

—The concept of a floor or superimposed "philanthropy tax" offends, in some eyes at least, the principle of voluntarism that is a cornerstone to philanthropy in the United States.

—The Conference Board survey of chief executive officers indicated that with a 1 per cent floor, 30 per cent of the executives would reduce or eliminate charitable giving and only 12 per cent of them would increase it. With a 2 per cent floor, 43 per cent of the executives said they would reduce or eliminate charitable giving and 17 per cent would increase it. Since 90 per cent of the companies in the survey gave below the 2 per cent level, 62 per cent below the 1 per cent level and 25 per cent below the 0.5 per cent level, it appears likely that the 2 per cent floor would significantly curtail giving and the 1 per cent floor would also result in reduced giving.

—With respect to the credit, half of the executives felt that corporate giving would increase if the tax system resulted in a lower "after-tax cost" than the present 100 per cent deduction. However, the majority of corporations are already at the 48 per cent marginal tax rate; charitable contributions "cost" them only 52 cents on the dollar. Therefore, many Commission members feel that an additional 10 per cent credit for corporate giving would be hard to justify on grounds of equity.

—A further finding from The Conference Board's survey of

executives indicated that tax incentives may be a relatively minor determinant of corporate giving compared to profit levels and a company's overall philosophy concerning giving and social responsibility.

A sizable minority of Commission members felt that despite the uncertainties and philosophical ambiguities that surround tax inducements to greater corporate giving, some such inducement should be instituted. But a majority of the Commission concluded that none of the tax alternatives studied by the Commission was both clearly effective enough and sufficiently in tune with the spirit and philosophy of philanthropy so as to merit the Commission's endorsement.

The Commission feels, however, that corporate giving can be significantly enlarged and improved by the leadership influence and example of corporations with generous, thoughtful and innovative programs that have set and hopefully will continue to set the pace for their industries and for the corporate world as a whole. The Commission commends and encourages such leadership. As recommended in the following chapter, the Commission also believes fuller disclosure requirements should include corporate giving, and that they will be beneficial in improving the quality of such giving.

Finally, the Commission hopes that its own encouragement of greater corporate giving will have some effect. It is ironic at least that the business community, which has so often expressed its wariness of Washington and the growing size of government, should fall so far short of legal limits in helping select and support publicly beneficial programs outside of government, through nonprofit charitable organizations. Former President Johnson recognized this irony in 1971 when he chided a group of business leaders about not contributing more to charity. "In spite of the fact that your federal government has seen fit to allow a charitable deduction of 5 per cent of your profits," he said, "the record is quite clear that you business leaders still feel that the federal government can spend this money more wisely than you can."

Recommendation

The record of giving by the corporate world as a whole in the mid-1970's is, the Commission feels, still quite clear, and it is ultimately an unimpressive and inadequate one. In the conviction that corporate giving both can and should be substantially increased, the Commission recommends:

That corporations set as a minimum goal, to be reached no later than 1980, the giving to charitable purposes of 2 per cent of pretax net income. Moreover, the Commission believes that the national commission proposed in this report should consider as a priority concern additional measures to stimulate corporate giving. *

*See comments by FRANCES T. FARENTHOLD, page 210, by GRACIELA OLIVAREZ, page 210, and by WILLIAM M. ROTH, page 211.

Sources for Chapter VI

R. Palmer Baker Jr. and J. Edward Shillingburg, *Corporate Charitable Contributions.**

Michael J. Boskin, *Estate Taxation and Charitable Bequests.**

Michael J. Boskin and Martin S. Feldstein, *Effects of the Charitable Deduction on Contributions by Low Income and Middle Income Households: Evidence from the National Survey of Philanthropy.**

Gerard M. Brannon, *A Pro-Charity Substitute for the Present Tax Law Treatment of Appreciated Property Contributed to Charity.**

Martin S. Feldstein, *Charitable Bequests, Estate Taxation and Intergenerational Wealth Transfers.**

Martin S. Feldstein, *Tax Incentives and Charitable Contributions in the United States: A Microeconometric Analysis.**

Martin S. Feldstein, *Estimating Separate Price Elasticities by Income Class.**

Martin S. Feldstein and Amy Taylor, *The Income Tax and Charitable Contributions: Estimates and Simulations with the Treasury Tax Files.**

James F. Harris and Anne Klepper, *Corporate Philanthropic Public Service Activities.**

C. Lowell Harriss, *Corporate Giving: Rationale, Issues and Opportunities.**

Theodore A. Kurz and Barbara P. Robinson, *Explanation and Analysis of Split Interest Gifts to Charity.**

Harry K. Mansfield and Ronald L. Groves, *Legal Aspects of Charitable Contributions of Appreciated Property to Public Charities.**

Paul R. McDaniel, *Study of Federal Matching Grants for Charitable Contributions.**

James N. Morgan, Richard F. Dye and Judith H. Hybels, *Results from Two National Surveys of Philanthropic Activity.**

Milton Moskowitz, *Corporate Charitable Contributions and Corporate Social Responsibility.**

John Holt Myers, *Estate Tax Deduction for Charitable Benefits: Proposed Limitations.**

Thomas Vasquez, *Corporate Giving Measurements.**

Richard E. Wagner, *Death, Taxes and Charitable Bequests: A Survey of Issues and Options.**

David Westfall, *Proposed Limitations on the Estate Tax Deduction for Charitable Transfers.**

Aaron Wildavsky and David Good, *A Tax by Any Other Name: The Donor Directed Automatic Percentage Contribution Bonus, A Budget Alternative for Financing Governmental Support of Charity.**

*Denotes reports and studies undertaken for the Commission.

VII

IMPROVING THE
PHILANTHROPIC PROCESS

One of the conventional wisdoms of the 1970's is that virtually all institutions, public and private, have declined in popular esteem and trust, especially those that exercise substantial economic or political power. The Presidency and Congress have consistently been given low ratings in public opinion polls in recent years. So have corporations, labor unions, the press.

A major source of this skepticism is said to be the widespread feeling that our institutions are beyond society's control, that they are operating for their own purposes which are often at odds with the public interest.

The third sector has fared better, perhaps, than the other two in the public's lowered estimations. In all likelihood, most Americans rarely think about philanthropy and nonprofit organizations in general terms but they probably do have attitudes about specific, mainly local voluntary groups such as the Boy Scouts or activities such as a church fund-raising drive, and these attitudes are probably positive on the whole. Moreover, unease about the giant, impersonal institutions of business and government may be serving to increase the appeal of the generally less giant, less impersonal institutions of the nonprofit sector.

All the same, it is likely that the sector's institutions are included to some degree in Americans' doubts. Indeed, voluntary sector institutions would appear to be particularly susceptible to concerns about control, about whether the public interest is truly being served. This is so because, while there are clear, widely acknowledged processes by which government and business institutions *should* be subject to incentives and restraints that lead them to serve the interests of society, it is not readily apparent what process, if any, is guiding nonprofit activity so that it benefits society.

159

Government, in theory at least, is subject to the whole apparatus of democracy, including representative legislatures, the electoral process and the vote. In the case of the business world, there is the competitive market place and the principles of profit-maximization and consumer sovereignty which are supposed to guide commerce toward a socially optimum production of goods and services. While some of the current disillusionment may reflect a lack of confidence in these processes—including a feeling that the processes can be and are manipulated by the very interests they are supposed to control—at least the processes are generally well understood and subject to examination for malfunctions, for reforms or replacements.

But in the case of nonprofit institutions and of philanthropy, there has never been a mechanism as simple, as comprehensible, in theory at least, as voting or buying that is supposed to keep this area in tune with public purposes. Foundations have been a particular object of wariness for just this reason, because they are thought to be able to exercise considerable economic power and political power while at the same time they appear to be subject to few built-in economic or political constraints. To a lesser degree perhaps, other nonprofit institutions may also appear to operate with few constraints: they have neither the market place nor the voting booth to answer to, or at least not so fully or directly as do businesses or government. The very freedom from such inhibitions that makes nonprofit organizations a valuable pluralistic addition to the commercial and political sectors, in other words, also makes them potentially suspect—perhaps, in today's suspicious atmosphere, more so than ever.*

Whether the public's skepticism and even cynicism about its institutions is well founded or not is, of course, a matter for and of considerable debate—and meantime even the best institutions may suffer along with the worst. Yet if this is a widely shared skepticism, as social analysts and attitude probers assure us it is, then it is a social reality in its own right and our institutions cannot fail to heed it and must respond to it, both for their own survival and for maintaining their usefulness to society. Accordingly, because this Commission believes that the

*See comment by MAX M. FISHER, page 211.

160

third sector should be encouraged and strengthened in its pluralistic role in American life, a major concern of the Commission is how to maintain, and if need be build, public trust in the sector and its institutions.

The proposals that the Commission has considered in this regard revolve around ideas of openness, of accountability, of accessibility—of, in so many words, making the inner workings of these institutions more visible, their decisions more public and more clearly responsive to the public needs and social change. These proposals are not unlike means that have been attempted or suggested in recent years for building public confidence in governmental and commercial institutions. But they may be all the more important for the world of voluntary organizations and philanthropy, because they are at the heart of a process that does, after all, exist to guide this world toward filling public needs.

This process is subtle and not as fully explored as are the processes of market economics and democratic politics. Still, there is a give and take, with elements both of economics and politics, that does guide—and ultimately restrain—the third sector. For this process to work well, in terms of filling social needs, there must be as much openness, as much give and take as functionally possible. There must be freedom of access for those seeking funds, for instance, to make known their needs and to attempt to persuade fund providers of the priority of these needs. There must be a free flow of information between donor and donee, between voluntary groups and the public at large, including government, between fund-solicitors and the public.* There must also be a wide range of choice for those who give time and money, as to where they will give and why. And there must be a genuine willingness to consider new avenues and new goals.

Yet much of the Commission's research, including meetings with and reports from representatives of donee organizations, indicates that the process is operating imperfectly at best.*

The need exists, in other words, both to make the philanthropic system work better and to assure the public that it is working in the public interest, and is therefore worthy of the public's trust. To the extent that many third sector institutions

*See comments by MAX M. FISHER, page 212.

serve increasingly as channels for public spending, it is not only public trust they must warrant but public money. As noted earlier in this report, growing government support of nonprofit activities is in itself a spur to greater openness and public accountability than many voluntary organizations have exercised, or felt obliged to exercise, in the past.

This growing role of government in relation to nonprofit organizations and activities also underlies what the Commission believes is an increasingly important function in the philanthropic process. This is the role of nonprofit organizations in trying to assist in the development of good public policy by various means including trying to influence legislation affecting their areas of concern. Yet as noted in Chapter I, organizations that devote a "substantial" amount of their resources to legislative activities are not eligible to receive deductible gifts. This restriction, the Commission believes, constitutes a severe and unwarranted limitation on the philanthropic process and on its effective functioning in our society.

With the foregoing considerations in mind, the Commission recommends specific steps toward improving the philanthropic process. These recommendations are put forward in this chapter within four broad, overlapping categories: accountability of nonprofit organizations to the public; accessibility by the public to these organizations; steps to minimize personal or institutional self-benefiting; and freedom of nonprofit groups to influence legislation. The proposals in these areas are offered with an eye above all to making the nonprofit sector function more effectively and more responsively in the public interest, both for the sake of this effectiveness and responsiveness and to insure the confidence of Americans in this, we believe, both worthy and essential array of institutions.

ACCOUNTABILITY

"There is a growing demand for more accountability on the part of private nonprofit institutions." This assertion in a report to the Commission on higher education is echoed in various forms throughout Commission studies as well as in recent pronouncements at large. The demand for accountability has been heard equally and perhaps even more strongly of late in connection with public and profit-making institutions, demands that range from stockholder calls for more communication from corporate managers to activists' political and legal battles to force more openness in the decision-making of government agencies, to legislation requiring greater disclosure of political campaign spending practices and sources. The pressures for greater accountability, however imprecise that term may be, have grown in recent years in the nonprofit sector as well, where, in addition to reflecting a general concern about the accountability of institutions they reflect conditions affecting the nonprofit sector in particular, including:

—The loose and even haphazard procedures that some nonprofit organizations employ to make themselves accountable to the public.*

—The increasing use of public funds by nonprofit organizations.

—The perception, on the part of certain segments of the population, that many private nonprofit organizations are too private, that they answer only to themselves or to each other. This viewpoint was encountered recurrently in Commission studies of philanthropy in five American cities and in several Commission-held meetings of representatives of "social action" groups—the notion of a closeknit philanthropic "establishment" in which a select group of donors and donees tended to be accountable mainly to each other. "The whole thing is like a private club," said a fund raiser in Cleveland.*

The pressure for greater accountability was translated into legislation in 1969 when Congress enacted, along with other related measures, a law requiring that all private foundations prepare annual reports and that these reports be filed with the IRS and with state authorities and be available to the general public. These annual reports were prescribed as supplements to information forms long required of tax-exempt organizations. Other kinds of accountability have been increasingly required by local, state and federal agencies as a condition of specific

*See comments by MAX M. FISHER, page 212.

grants to specific nonprofit organizations.

Yet the Commission feels that, while many voluntary organizations have on their own initiative made themselves highly accountable in various ways, the overall level of accountability in the voluntary sector is inadequate. The 1969 reporting regulations for foundations have been honored, the evidence suggests, with bare minimal compliance in some cases as far as easy availability of annual reports goes. Information forms that current IRS regulations require of tax-exempt organizations ask for only a limited kind of information, have been difficult to get hold of through the government, and, a report to the Commission finds, may be several years old by the time they can be examined by the public. Accountings required by various governmental grantors on the other hand have been relatively narrowly oriented—as they should be—toward specific uses of such funds rather than the overall operations of the grantees. And a Commission-initiated study by state attorneys general indicates that other state disclosure requirements are incomplete and uneven at best.

Recommendations

The Commission therefore recommends:

1. *That all larger tax-exempt charitable organizations except churches and church affiliates be required to prepare and make readily available detailed annual reports on their finances, programs and priorities.* *

Reporting requirements that now apply only to private foundations should be broadened so that all 501(c)(3) and 501(c)(4) organizations with annual budgets of more than $100,000 are required to file annual reports. This requirement would not apply to religious organizations, although some Commission members feel that it should apply to nonsacramental activities of religious organizations such as hospitals and schools. But the requirement is meant to include the tax-deductible charitable spending of business corporations; any corporation whose contributions came to $100,000 or more a

*See comment by ELIZABETH J. McCORMACK, page 213.

164

year would be required to file annual reports on these contributions.

Every tax-exempt organization's or corporation's report would have to be filed with appropriate state and federal agencies and, in addition, be made directly and swiftly available, at or below cost, to any person or organization upon request. The permanent commission on the nonprofit sector, recommended in Chapter VIII, could facilitate this process.

Each report should include at least the following information:

—Name, address, purpose and founding date of the organization;

—Names of trustees or directors or other governing persons;

—Names and titles of paid officers;

—Description of program and priorities, explanation of the criteria that are taken into account in accepting or rejecting requests for funds, products or services and, if the organization is a foundation, a list of grants made in the previous year, their recipients, purposes and amounts;

—Financial information, including:

A statement of income, including sources and amounts;

A statement of expenditures including adminstrative expenditures;

A balance sheet;

A list of investments held;

An opinion of independent auditors.

Uniform Accounting Measures

As an important element in better, more communicative financial accountability, the Commission urges that uniform accounting measures be adopted by comparable nonprofit organizations. One obstacle in the path of accountability is the tangle of accounting definitions and principles that are in effect among nonprofit organizations, which makes examination of any particular organization's basic finances often difficult if not impossible, especially for nonexperts, and compounds the problems of comparing one organization with another.

Because of the wide range of activities and kinds of organizations involved in the nonprofit sector, the Commission recognizes that it may not be possible to apply uniform accounting practices throughout the nonprofit sector. However, greater uniformity, at least among comparable types of organizations, is clearly possible and desirable. The Commission recognizes that some important steps in this direction have been taken in recent years but feels that considerable further progress remains to be made.* A Commission advisory committee on accounting practices has developed a model accounting form for nonprofit organizations. Consideration of this form, which is in the compendium of Commission research, and of the principles behind it, is recommended to nonprofit organizations.

The Commission applauds the many exempt organizations that on their own initiative and from their own sense of accountability regularly disclose significantly more about their operations, their revenues and expenditures than is required by law, and it urges all tax-exempt organizations to heed these examples.

2. *That larger grant-making organizations be required to hold annual public meetings to discuss their programs, priorities and contributions.*

The Commission believes that individual organizations and the nonprofit sector as a whole would benefit from direct exposure of grant-making organizations to their immediate constituency and to the public at large. As in the Commission's recommendation on reporting above, this requirement would exclude religious organizations and include corporate givers that make annual grants or contributions of $100,000 or more. Also included would be federated fund-raising organizations—such as United Ways. Meetings would be held in the city in which the principal office of the organization is located. Adequate notice would be provided in a publication of general circulation.

3. *That the present 4 per cent "audit" tax on private foundations be repealed and replaced by a fee on all private foundations based on the total actual costs of auditing them.***

The present tax on foundations, imposed by the 1969 Tax

*See comment by MAX M. FISHER, page 213.
**See dissent by ALAN PIFER, page 214.

166

Reform Act, should be changed for two reasons, the Commission believes. First, the tax produces receipts which far exceed the expenditures of IRS in auditing tax-exempt organizations. From 1971 through 1973, the tax raised $157 million whereas IRS costs for auditing tax-exempt organizations for these three years amounted to only $55 million. Second, the tax constitutes a levy not on foundations but on the entire donee population, and on all its beneficiaries, because money that is taxed from foundations is unavailable for grants to donees.

Therefore, the Commission proposes instead an audit fee based on the actual costs of auditing private foundations alone. The fee, set as a percentage of income, would be adjusted periodically according to estimates of such costs over a future span, say of five years. The fee would not apply to other tax-exempt organizations, and the costs of their audits would be borne by general government revenues.

4. *That the Internal Revenue Service continue to be the principal agency responsible for the oversight of tax-exempt organizations.* *

The Commission has considered numerous proposals to substitute another agency for the Internal Revenue Service in overseeing the affairs of exempt organizations. Among the reasons given for an alternate agency was the greater assurance of insulation of the nonprofit sector from political or executive branch interference. The Commission was not persuaded that a viable alternate to the Internal Revenue Service exists and was, in fact, satisfied that, except in several isolated instances, the Service has demonstrated its capacity for independent, impartial oversight of tax-exempt organizations including determination of exempt status.

ACCESSIBILITY

A corollary to greater accountability by nonprofit organizations is the aim of making voluntary organizations more open, more accessible, to a wide range of viewpoints. This goal is

*See dissents by GRACIELA OLIVAREZ, page 214, and by FRANCES T. FARENTHOLD, page 214.

barely separable from that of accountability. Disclosure requirements recommended here in the name of accountability would also serve the cause of accessibility, by providing guidance to those who attempt to influence or to seek assistance from nonprofit organizations. Public meetings would serve as forums not only for communication outward from an organization's leadership but, inevitably, for challenging and attempted persuasion by those seeking access inward to the organization's attention and resources.

Greater accessibility has frequently been espoused as a goal in the nonprofit world, yet the evidence suggests that it is often honored more in preachments than in practice, particularly in regard to unconventional groups and viewpoints. In the course of the Commission's examinations, a number of meetings were held around the country that brought representatives of such groups, who generally depend on outside sources of support, together with donor representatives, a form of donee-donor encounter that the Commission hopes will be continued and broadened in the future. The complaint was repeatedly heard at these meetings that philanthropic institutions—foundations and federated fund-raising organizations in particular*—tended to erect barriers to easy access by those bringing unfamiliar pleas for unconventional or controversial causes. The "pioneering" role of the voluntary sector, it was charged, is frustrated by closed doors and closed minds.**

Such complaints have been sounded in particular by "social action" or "public interest" groups and by women's activist organizations who say their causes are going underfunded, in part because of what they claim is the inaccessibility of many philanthropic institutions. This inaccessibility tends to result, they charge, in the following of established patterns of giving to established donee areas and institutions. The result: "We believe that instead of being the venture capital for social change," states a "Donee Group" report to the Commission, "philanthropy has, for the most part, patterned itself after its corporate and governmental counterparts. It has become bureaucratic, safe and more conservative and less willing to take

*See comment by FRANCES T. FARENTHOLD, page 216.
**See comment by MAX M. FISHER, page 217.

risks than the relatively inflexible government to which it is so closely related."

The Commission is concerned that the philanthropic process may not be fluid enough to respond to new needs as they emerge and are perceived. And we take note that charges of insufficient accessibility to both the ears and treasuries of institutionalized philanthropic sources are made not only by new groups with new causes to promote but are also acknowleged by longer established organizations within the philanthropic world.

The Commission feels further that greater accessibility to funding organizations by all segments of society, with their differing perceptions of needs, can only enrich the philanthropic process and ensure that in aggregate it is tending to public needs that best are served by the voluntary sector's particular capabilities. The Commission believes that private giving should be constantly aware of and sympathetic to emerging needs, particularly of groups and causes in society that are least able to meet their own needs. This is one of the traditional missions of "philanthropy" and of "charity" and it continues today with different thrusts and perspectives. Therefore private donors, whether individuals, corporations, or foundations, should fully inform themselves of such needs and examine their present funding priorities in the light of these needs, and they should do so with a sense of obligation, both to themselves and to the changing society in which they live.

Recommendations

With the aim of encouraging and facilitating wider access to and greater venturesomeness by institutional philanthropy, the Commission recommends:

1. *That the duplication of legal responsibility for proper expenditure of foundation grants, now imposed on both foundations and recipients, be eliminated and that recipient organizations be made primarily responsible for their expenditures.*

Under the 1969 tax reform measures, foundations and their officers became legally accountable, through "expenditure re-

169

sponsibility" and reporting provisions, for the actions of groups they aided. This, the Commission believes, serves as an undesirable and unnecessary restraint on the openness and venturesomeness of foundations. "Expenditure responsibility" also imposes heavy legal and administrative burdens, particularly on smaller and newer organizations.

The Commission believes that the "expenditure responsibility" requirement as now imposed on foundations not only duplicates responsibility by placing requirements on both the grantor and the grantee, but unduly enhances the power of foundations over grantees. It puts foundations in a policing and surveillance role and thus undermines the autonomy of grantee organizations. This responsbility should rest on the grantees. The Commission believes that abuses that gave rise to the "expenditure responsibility" requirement are adequately contained under the Commission's recommendations for greater accountability by all nonprofit organizations, by other provisions of the 1969 Act, and by legal remedies outside the act.

2. *That tax-exempt organizations, particularly funding organizations, recognize an obligation to be responsive to changing viewpoints and emerging needs and that they take steps such as broadening their boards and staffs to insure that they are responsive.**

Charitable nonprofit organizations exist and enjoy special tax status to serve public purposes, one of which, as this report earlier recognizes, is to act as pioneers of social change. Therefore, the Commission believes that such organizations, especially those that serve to channel funds to other nonprofit groups, have a public obligation, which transcends their private prerogatives, to be aware of and responsive to new attitudes and needs of all segments of society.

One means of attempting to meet this obligation, a means that the Commission feels exempt organizations should periodically employ, is to deliberately examine and if need be broaden their boards and staffs so that a wide range of viewpoints is reflected in each organization's very governance and manage-

*See comments by FRANCES T. FARENTHOLD, page 217, by GRACIELA OLIVAREZ, page 219, by WILLIAM M. ROTH, page 219, by MAX M. FISHER, page 220.

ment. Exempt organizations, like other institutions in our society, should be especially aware of the importance of having participation—more than token participation—of minority groups and women in their governance and management.

The Commission has considered and rejected the principle that all voluntary organization boards be "representative" of the public at large or of any particular community. A principal virtue of the nonprofit sector is that it reflects different priorities, differently arrived at, than does representative government. To impose representativeness on the control of voluntary organizations would, the Commission believes, undermine an important distinction between the voluntary sector and government.

However, unless repeated steps are taken by charitable organizations to diversify board memberships, the possibility must be envisaged of "public members" being imposed on the boards of these organizations. In any case, as government funds increasingly flow into or through voluntary organizations, they may have to give more consideration themselves to inviting "public members" on their boards as an element of public access and control. Methods of naming such members and the implications for the governance of nonprofit organizations are subjects that should be studied by the permanent commission on the nonprofit sector recommended in Chapter VIII.

Not only does the Commission urge and encourage the broadening of viewpoints in the staffing and directing of existing nonprofit organizations, but it urges the establishment of new organizations and new organizational structures that broaden the spectrum of institutional philanthropy in general.

Within the last several years, for instance, a number of new foundations with strikingly unconventional funding priorities have sprung up. A "People's Trust," which would raise funds in modest monthly pledges for projects in Atlanta's poorer neighborhoods is currently being explored. The Commission applauds such developments and feels that the philanthropic world should be receptive to more of them.

The Commission also suggests the wide use of intermediary organizations that provide centralized professional services to nascent groups in their dealings with foundations, groups that

171

are unaccustomed to the process of seeking and managing foundation grants. Further, in the name of wider geographical as well as social accessibility, the Commission believes that the largest foundations, most of which are situated in major eastern cities, should consider means for making themselves more aware of, and accessible to, groups in other parts of the country.

3. *That a new category of "independent" foundation be established by law. Such organizations would enjoy the tax benefits of public charities in return for diminished influence on the foundation's board by the foundation's benefactor or by his or her family or business associates.**

Linked to most Commission research on and discussion of the subject of broadening foundation boards has been the issue of "donor control" of private foundations. Traditionally, after a foundation is established, the giver of the foundation's endowment plays an active role in its running or if, as is often the case, the foundation grows out of a bequest, the bequeather's family and associates play such a role. The question has been raised intermittently in the philanthropic world and by critical observers of this world as to whether there should be some limitation on this control. The question is raised in terms of social equity: In view of the important role of favorable tax laws in the creation of foundations, should the founder, through offspring, relatives or associates, be allowed an indefinite role in the control of a foundation? The question is also raised as a matter of access: Is a donor-controlled foundation likely to reflect a particularly narrow perspective, to be inaccessible to a range of viewpoints?

The Commission feels that there is no clear-cut answer to either question, which involves complex value judgments, insufficient data and such related imponderables as whether limiting donor control would discourage the setting up of new foundations. Any questions about donor control must take account of the fact that some donor-controlled foundations are widely regarded as being among the most innovative and effective of philanthropic organizations. Therefore, the Commission does not recommend any specific limitation of donor control,

*See comment by WILLIAM M. ROTH, page 220.

172

but urges considerable further examination of the issue, while espousing the general view that openness and accessibility are as important for donor-controlled foundations as for other philanthropic, nonprofit organizations. If, in any particular organization, relinquishing a degree of donor control serves to further the cause of greater accessibility, then this course should, we feel, be positively pursued.

To counterbalance whatever disincentives there may be to relinquishing full donor control and because it sees a positive value in broadening the decision-making base of foundations, the Commission recommends the establishment of a new category of "independent" foundations. Governing boards of such foundations would be restricted to at most a minority representation by the donor, the donor's family and business associates. In return, such organizations would not be subject to the limitations on giving that now apply to private foundations, including the ceiling of 20 per cent of a giver's income that can be deducted from income taxes for gifts to private foundations, the restriction against endowment gifts from income of other foundations and the exclusion from full eligibility to receive appreciated property that is deductible at market price.

MINIMIZING PERSONAL OR INSTITUTIONAL SELF-BENEFITING

Part of the basic definition, written into law, of the tax-exempt organizations that have been the focus of the Commission's examination is that no share of such organizations' net earnings may benefit private shareholders or individuals. More popularly put, nonprofit organizations are not in business to make money for anyone and if they do, they shouldn't be allowed tax exemptions but should be subject to the same levies as ordinary commercial organizations.

Yet a few situations have been uncovered and have been highly publicized in which nonprofit organizations or specific transactions within such organizations have clearly served above all to benefit managers, benefactors or others associated with the organizations, or simply have led to the enrichment of an organization itself with no increase in the organization's benefits to society. Most widely disparaged, perhaps, has been the finding that a few organizations, because of extraordinary inefficiency as well as self-benefiting, have spent more on fund raising and administrative costs than on the purpose for which they raised funds and were presumably in existence. In some cases, less than one out of five dollars has remained for an organization's ostensible operating purposes.

Over the years, other abuses that have offended the spirit of the law that gives special tax privileges to nonprofit organizations have come to public attention, including charitable organizations established and maintained primarily to purchase the products of commercial manufacturers, to be given away in the process of soliciting funds; less-than-arms-length dealings between charitable organizations and businesses with which their officers or directors are connected, resulting in unconscionable benefits to the individual involved, or in losses to the organization because it did not bargain for goods or services in the open market; and unreasonable compensation to officers and employees.

As a result of Congress's investigations of foundations in 1969, prompted by some dramatic examples of abuse, laws were passed specifically aimed at eliminating such abuses by private foundations. The Commission believes that tax-exempt organizations other than private foundations may be as open to the possibility of such abuses, however, and therefore it favors extension to other exempt organizations, at least in part and with appropriate modifications, of several of the 1969 prohibitions that now apply only to private foundations. The Commission also believes that other remedies and restraints are called for to insure public confidence that charitable nonprofit organizations do indeed serve only charitable nonprofit causes.

Recommendations

The Commission therefore recommends:

1. *That all tax-exempt organizations be required by law to maintain "arms-length" business relationships with profit-making*

organizations or activities in which any member of the organization's staff, any board member or any major contributor has a substantial financial interest, either directly or through his or her family.

An outright prohibition against business dealings between a nonprofit organization and individuals or companies to which principals in the nonprofit organization are linked was considered by the Commission and rejected as not practical for all voluntary organizations. Such a prohibition, it was felt, could put many voluntary organizations at a considerable disadvantage, particularly local operating charities that would not be able to do business with a local bank or real estate firm or a supplier, even on specially favorable terms, if the business were owned or managed by a trustee or officer of the voluntary organizations. Yet, in addition to the "arms-length" requirement, all transactions should be prohibited where they result in financial injury to the organization; any improper benefits should be recoverable through action by state or federal authorities; and appropriate penalties should be provided.

2. *That to discourage unnecessary accumulation of income, a flat payout rate of 5 per cent of principal be fixed by Congress for private foundations and a lower rate for other endowed tax-exempt organizations.**

Present law requires that private foundations make annual disbursements for their exempt purposes of a percentage of the organization's endowment. The percentage is fixed by the Secretary of the Treasury and varies with interest rates and investment yields throughout the economy. Because of circumstances in the financial market place, the payout rate (now set at 6 per cent) is higher, by a significant degree, than the yield that can be anticipated from a balanced investment portfolio. The effect of this payout requirement has been to cause foundations to invade capital beyond any reasonable expectations of long-term capital appreciation that might cover such invasions.

The Commission strongly supports the principle of the required "payout," not only for private foundations, but also for all exempt organizations with endowment resources. But the

*See dissent by WILLIAM M. ROTH, page 220.

payout rate should not be so high as to cause erosion of endowment funds. Nor does the Commission view the short-term fluctuations in the rate, now occurring under present law, to be desirable. A flat payout rate of 5 per cent would assure the adequacy of continuing charitable payments, yet would permit well-planned management of the organization's endowment funds. Because financial circumstances may change over time, the 5 per cent rate could be set for a fixed period, such as five years, and reviewed by the Congress at the end of that period.

Public charities are not currently subject to any payout requirement, and at least one well publicized instance has come to light in which a charitable organization has amassed large financial holdings while doing little to expand its charitable activities. So the Commission believes that a payout rule is desirable for other endowed charities as well as for foundations. For organizations other than private foundations, however, the payout rate should be set at a smaller percentage and it should be satisfied by the use of funds for the direct conduct of the organization's activities, including the acquisition, construction or repair of buildings or other facilities, the acquisition of art objects by museums and so forth. Accumulations, in fact, should be liberally allowed for purposes that clearly further the organization's tax-exempt functions and services.

The provisions of the present law that prevent a private foundation from making speculative or other investments which "jeopardize its exempt purposes" should also be applied, with appropriate modifications, to all exempt organizations.

3. *That a system of federal regulation be established for interstate charitable solicitations and that intrastate solicitations be more effectively regulated by state governments.**

In the Commission's sample survey of taxpayers, 30 per cent of those questioned said they did not like the way their contributions were used and one out of seven respondents specifically complained of excessive fund-raising or administrative costs. This wariness undoubtedly has been heightened in many minds by recent cases, including those uncovered in congressional investigations, where some costs of charitable fund rais-

*See dissent by RAYMOND J. GALLAGHER, page 220.

ing absorbed most of the funds raised, leaving the impression that some charitable solicitations are more for the benefit of the solicitors than for the charitable causes involved. In some other instances, contributions have been recurrently solicited and raised that are far in excess of the organization's operating outlays.

The Commission believes that the vast majority of charitable solicitations are conscientiously and economically undertaken. Nonetheless, cases of unduly costly or needless fund raising point to the absence of any focused mechanism for overseeing such activity and, if need be, applying sanctions. One Commission study finds, in fact, that only one half of the 50 states regulated the solicitation of funds and that "the coverage and scope of" those that do regulate "vary widely." State regulation of intrastate solicitations, the Commission believes, should be strengthened, but because many solicitations spread over many states at once, state regulation is inevitably limited in its effectiveness. Clearly, the federal government and federal law must play the major role in assuring the integrity of charitable solicitations, a role that they just as clearly do not play today.

The Commission recommends specifically that all charitable organizations should be required by law to disclose all solicitation costs to the Internal Revenue Service, in accordance with accepted accounting principles; that all solicitation literature should be required to carry a notice to the effect that full financial data can be obtained from the soliciting organization on request; that any such requests be required to be rapidly answered; and that a special office be established in the Internal Revenue Service or in some other federal agency or regulatory body, such as the Federal Trade Commission, to oversee charity solicitation and take action against improper, misleading or excessively costly fund raisings. This special office might be supplemented by and guided by an accrediting organization, which would review the finances of and certify all exempt organizations whose solicitation practices are found to merit approval.

The Commission considered but rejected proposals that solicitation costs be legally limited to a fixed percentage of receipts because, unless such a ceiling were so high as to be an

177

ineffective restraint on most fund raising, it would risk being too low to account for the often justifiably high costs of solicitation for new or unpopular causes. On the other hand, state as well as federal agencies concerned with regulating solicitations should be required to establish clear qualitative criteria as to what constitutes "excessively costly" fund raising (or improper or misleading solicitation, as well). Such criteria should be widely publicized so that both soliciting organizations and the contributing public would clearly understand the limits within which fund raisers operate.

4. *That as a federal enforcement tool against abuses by tax-exempt organizations, and to protect these organizations themselves, sanctions appropriate to the abuses should be enacted as well as forms of administrative or judicial review of the principal existing sanction—revocation of an organization's exempt status.*

Removal of tax exemption, which for many nonprofit organizations would mean closing their doors, is much too blunt a weapon against charitable abuses, and for this reason is highly ineffective; the government hesitates to use it. On the other hand, when it is used, judicial challenges are slow and costly, and because an organizaton may not be able to survive in the meantime without exempt status, revoking an exemption can be, in effect, an unappealable penalty.

Therefore the Commission believes that more moderate sanctions need be devised as well as swift appeal processes. Among the sanctions envisioned are those that the government could apply to organizations whose activities go beyond their exempt purposes or to organizations whose activities would be penalized under the Commission's recommendation on arms-length dealing. Among the appeal processes, there should be both administrative and judicial means of appeal. Of the latter, the Commission advocates procedures whereby an exempt organization may ask a federal court for a declaratory judgment on its tax-exempt status or its eligibility to receive tax-deductible gifts. During litigation or appeal involving either sanctions or determination of tax status, an exempt organization should generally be allowed to continue its charitable operations. Present laws prevent an appeal when the IRS denies or fails to act on an application for exempt status. So appeal procedures should apply to initial determination of tax-exempt status as well as to revocation of this status.

INFLUENCING LEGISLATION

The relationship between the nonprofit sector and government is both complementary and competitive. On the one hand, the two sectors often perform related functions in various areas of society, at times and places relying on each other's assistance and co-existing in relative harmony.

On the other hand, as Chapter I has noted, a degree of tension and conflict, not necessarily unhealthy or socially unbeneficial, has marked relations between government and voluntary organizations and associations throughout history.

The ambivalence of this relationship is perhaps most clearly reflected today in the fact that for nearly six decades government has, through the charitable deduction, encouraged a wide range of activity and influence by nonprofit organizations, and yet, for two thirds of that time, since 1934, it has specifically prohibited tax deductibility for any organization, a "substantial part of the activities of which" goes to "attempting to influence legislation." Government, in other words, encourages the nonprofit sector to do a great deal but specifically discourages it from trying to influence government itself.

Two principal rationales have been offered for this discouragement. The image has been evoked at various times of the corridors of Capitol Hill swarming with lobbyists operating with huge "slush funds" from nonprofit organizations.* The idea that tax immunity is a form of government subsidy is part of another argument: in this view government should not, but would, be in a position of subsidizing efforts to influence itself if it allowed tax-deductible organizations to lobby freely.

In recent years, however, there has been growing pressure to remove or relax the restrictions on attempting to influence legislation. This pressure has developed because of a number of factors:

*See comment by MAX M. FISHER, page 221.

—In 1962, Internal Revenue Code provisions covering business taxes were amended to allow a business to deduct the costs of influencing legislation affecting the direct interests of that business. Deduction of dues to trade associations that lobby on behalf of a business's industry-wide interests has been permitted under the amendment. Thus an inconsistency exists wherein businesses and trade associations are able to lobby for their interests and to benefit from tax deductions for the costs of such lobbying, but nonprofit organizations and associations are allowed considerably less freedom to lobby or otherwise attempt to influence legislation without endangering their tax-deductibility status.

—Considerable uncertainty surrounds just what constitutes a "substantial part" of an organization's activities or "attempting to influence legislation." After forty years of the tax-law provision, this uncertainty remains unclarified by either the courts or the Internal Revenue Service. One result is that some larger nonprofit groups are able to lobby amply within the law, because in relation to their size their legislative activities make up no substantial part of overall activities. Smaller groups, however, lobby at the risk of treading over some ill-defined line and thereby losing their special tax status; as a result, they may hesitate to engage in lobbying activities to any significant degree at all.

—Less directly but perhaps most profoundly affecting attitudes toward such restrictions on nonprofit organizations is the change in the relative sizes of government and the nonprofit sector in recent decades. As government has expanded in relation to the nonprofit sector, the influencing of government has tended to become an ever more important role of nonprofit organizations. As nonprofit organizations provide smaller shares of health, education and welfare services, for instance, the ability to influence the larger provider—government—becomes more important.

—"Public interest" and "social action" groups have been growing in numbers in the nonprofit sector; they may well represent a major new direction of the sector; and one of their foremost roles has been precisely to influence legislation. Some groups such as Common Cause and the League of Women

Voters have deliberately, if unhappily, adopted non-deductible status so as to be able to lobby without restraint. They feel that, while they are still able to enjoy tax-exempt status, the law should allow them to lobby and still to receive tax-deductible contributions.

—The Constitutional question has been raised as to whether this inhibition against influencing legislation is an infringement of free speech and of the right to petition government.

Pressures to change the anti-lobbying restriction have resulted in a number of proposals and congressional bills in recent years. The American Bar Assocation in 1969 passed a resolution that advocated amending the Internal Revenue Code to allow a nonprofit organization to lobby with respect to legislation that was of direct interest to the organization. This resolution became the basis for a Senate bill two years later and since then various bills have been drafted in Congress with wide differences but the similar goal of easing or more clearly defining, but not totally removing, the restrictions on nonprofit organizations against lobbying and other means of influencing legislation.

Recommendation

Against this background of a long-standing barrier between voluntary organizations and government, the Commission recommends:

That nonprofit organizations, other than foundations, be allowed the same freedoms to attempt to influence legislation as are business corporations and trade associations, that toward this end Congress remove the current limitation on such activity by charitable groups eligible to receive tax-deductible gifts.

The only major restrictions in this area that the Commission believes can be fully justified are:

Those that would prevent a person or group from being able to set up an organization to campaign for a particular piece of legislation and then deduct from income taxes the expenses of running such an operation. Therefore, the Commission recommends that organizations receiving tax-deductible gifts must be required to have broader charitable aims and functions apart from any immediate legislative activities.

Prohibitions against a nonprofit organization's supporting or opposing a candidate for public office.

Maintaining the current total prohibition against lobbying by private foundations.

Otherwise, the Commission believes that there should be no restrictions, linked to tax deductibility, on what the Commission feels has become an increasingly important role of the nonprofit sector and a major part of the philanthropic process.

Sources for Chapter VII

Accounting Advisory Committee, *A Study of the Inadequacies of Present Financial Reporting by Philanthropic Organizations.**

Thomas R. Asher, *Public Needs, Public Policy and Philanthropy.**

Msgr. Geno Baroni, Arthur Naparstek, Karen Kollias, *Patterns of Class and Ethnic Discrimination by Private Philanthropy.**

Sarah C. Carey, *Philanthropy and the Powerless.**

Council on Foundations, Inc., *Private Foundations and the 1969 Tax Reform Act.**

David Ginsburg, Lee R. Marks, Ronald P. Wertheim, *Federal Oversight of Private Philanthropy.**

Arthur Jack Grimes, *The Fund-Raising Percent as a Quantitative Standard for Regulation of Public Charities with Particular Emphasis on Voluntary Health and Welfare Organizations.**

John B. Huffaker, *Legislative Activities of Charitable Organizations Other than Private Foundations.**

Reynold Levy and Waldemar A. Nielsen, *An Agenda for the Future.**

Peter G. Meek, *Self-Regulation in Private Philanthropy.**

Phillip W. Moore, *Foundation Grants to Corporate Activist Groups: The Donee Perspective.**

Ohio Attorney General's Office, Charitable Foundations Section, *The Status of State Regulations of Charitable Trusts, Foundations and Solicitations.**

Peter J. Petkas, *The New Federalism, Government Accountability and Philanthropy.**

David Horton Smith, *Values, Voluntary Action and Philanthropy: The Appropriate Relationship of Private Philanthropy to Public Needs.**

Lawrence M. Stone, *The Charitable Foundation: Its Governance.**

Mary Jean Tully, *Who's Funding the Women's Movement?**

United States Human Resources Corporation, *Foundations' Responsiveness to Concerns of Minority Groups*, San Francisco, 1975.

*Denotes reports and studies undertaken for the Commission.

VIII

A PERMANENT COMMISSION

The Commission on Private Philanthropy and Public Needs has addressed itself to many of the issues, challenges, changes and simple uncertainties that face the third sector and its philanthropic underpinnings in the mid-1970's. The Commission's studies, we feel, have significantly advanced the state of knowledge in this area. Yet for every subject examined, it has become evident that many other subjects remain barely explored. For every conclusion, recommendation or finding involving any particular issue or set of issues, there has not been enough information to come to definitive conclusions about other important or pressing issues. Such is the immensity and diversity of this area of American life, and such has been the scarcity of information that has faced the Commission that we inevitably have had to leave depths unfathomed.

Why do people give? And, of equal importance, why do some not give even though their economic circumstances would make it feasible for them to do so? We still do not know in any easily analyzable or quantifiable sense.

What are the dimensions of "charitable" activity and of giving, and what are the characteristics and problems of the major categories of nonprofit institutions? "The lack of information is striking," notes a Commission report covering these areas. We have made estimates and extrapolations, but it is clear that they are only that; and as regards the economic condition of the third sector, in addition to suffering long-term economic strains, it has unquestionably been severely struck by the recent recession and inflation, but precise information about what can best be done to alleviate the crisis of some institutions is still lacking.

What are the purposes, the public needs, to which nonprofit organizations and philanthropic resources are best oriented? As this report observes in earlier parts, virtually the whole breadth of our social and cultural consciousness and activity is encom-

185

passed by philanthropy and nonprofit activity, from relief of hunger to support of the fine arts, from studies in biosociology to public television. There is no single set of priorities that applies across this whole immense range, no easy arranging or rearranging of the optimum distribution of philanthropic resources between various claimants within this range. This Commission itself has been divided, in fact, as any reasonably representative group might well be in the mid-1970's, on what is a socially optimum allocation of philanthropic resources, and on whether change in the present allocation is necessary or desirable.

Perhaps wisely, we have tended to limit our discussions to means rather than ends, to processes by which it is hoped that nonprofit activity and philanthropy can be both strengthened and guided toward addressing needs that society's third sector is best designed to fulfill. Yet, the Commission also recognizes that if private giving should continue to shrink in relation to the rest of the economy, and if nonprofit activity should continue to grow smaller in comparison with governmental parallels, the determination of the best uses of these voluntary resources may become a paramount and recurrent issue facing the nonprofit sector and American society as a whole.

As noted elsewhere in this report, the monitoring and influencing of government may be emerging as one of the most effective and socially beneficial roles of the voluntary sector, and perhaps philanthropic resources and the processes that encourage and direct these resources should in the future be more specifically oriented toward this role. Or perhaps it will become evident that the oversight of corporations should be given priority in the use of such resources, as corporations themselves loom ever larger not only in the economic but in the social life of America. Then, too, there are those who are already saying that giving in the voluntary sector should be refocused on a role that is as old as philanthropy and charity themselves—helping the helpless, or, as viewed in contemporary socio-political terms, empowering the powerless. What, then, of philanthropy's current major recipients and beneficiaries?

"One of the difficulties in assessing the functions of private philanthropy in America," as Robert J. Blendon, vice president

186

of the Robert Wood Johnson Foundation, writes in a Commission study, "is that, in a changing society, past experience may not be a reliable guide for interpreting correctly currents of future need." Accordingly, philanthropic priorities should become a matter of examination on a continuous basis.

Many other aspects of philanthropy need to be studied as well. Many questions remain to be answered, and many to be asked. Moreover, even the answers the Commission confidently offers today in areas to which it has given particular attention, such as the relationship of taxes to giving, are subject to change, perhaps with very little notice. For, above all, it is clear that the region we have explored is itself changing swiftly, perhaps profoundly.

Part of a Larger Process

So the Commission regards its efforts, its examinations and deliberations as but a modest beginning of what must become a larger and longer process if the voluntary sector and philanthropy are to become as well understood, as well mapped, as the government and business worlds. And they must be better understood, we feel, on a continuous and up-to-date basis, if they are to play their most productive role and to be intelligently guided in this role.

The scope and duration of the need is such that there should be established, in the view of the Commission, a new organization of recognized national stature and authority that will work steadily and on a long-term basis to strengthen the nonprofit sector and the practice of private giving for public purposes. Many areas within the sector have created associations to champion their causes and interests. But the sector as a whole, in part because of its very scale and diversity, has no single entity to give the kind of serious thought and attention to its overall and fundamental problems as traditionally have been given to the profit-making sector and to the structure and functioning of government.

Yet in a time when the sector is subject to both economic strains and political and philosophical questioning, when pro-

187

found changes are taking place in its role and in its relationship to government, and when philanthropy has failed to keep pace with society, in economic and financial terms at least, the Commission believes that such an entity is necessary for the growth, perhaps even the survival, of the sector as an effective instrument of individual initiative and social progress.

Among the major purposes of any such organization, in addition to attempting to find answers to the questions above, would be to study in depth the funding problems of nonprofit groups and the means of increasing the flow of private funds into these institutions. Alongside philanthropic giving, which has been the major financial area of concern of this Commission, operating revenues are the other principal source of private funds for nonprofit organizations, and study and development is needed of ways of increasing such revenues including ways of removing legal barriers to nonprofit organizations' earning operating revenues. Present IRS regulations, for instance, severely limit the capacity of public-interest law firms to earn legal fees for their services, fees that would go a long way toward making these kinds of nonprofit groups self-supporting.

In addition to private funding, any future body on the nonprofit sector will also inevitably have to concern itself with the growing role—and growing challenge—of government funding. A major task ahead is to study further and develop guidelines and insulating institutional channels for government funding that will accommodate government's right to be assured that public money is properly spent but will protect recipients of funds from stifling bureaucratic or political intrusion.

Indeed, the whole area of working relationships between government and the private nonprofit sector needs further attention and study—relationships that are increasingly complex, fluid, undefined and hazardous as government programs and budgets grow in areas of nonprofit activity. The terms of government contracts and grants, and the accountability and reporting requirements included can, and sometimes do, impose not only costs and burdens upon private agencies but even dangers to their constitutional rights. Government decisions to subsidize hospital construction or to make sudden slashes in the level of support for research programs can have unintended but nonetheless huge and damaging side-effects on private institutions that lie in the path of such new directions of public policy or that are dependent on government support for some of their programs.

The point has been reached where such impacts are not occasional or incidental but continuous and numerous as a result of legislative and executive branch decisions on budgetary, program and procedural matters at all levels, federal, state and local. And yet these impacts, which increasingly define the role and determine the viability of large categories of the third sector, are neither anticipated nor systematically identified and evaluated in the processes of legislative and administrative policy making.

There is need therefore for the invention and establishment of a new kind of entity to fill this great and dangerous void. It must be a permanent and not temporary agency; it must have "critical mass" in the scale of its financing; it must have both great stature and independence, to exercise significant influence at the same time upon the private nonprofit sector, upon public attitudes and understanding, and upon both the legislative and executive branches of government. It must be simultaneously a center for the study and analysis of problems, for the formulation of constructive proposals for their solution by both private and public elements, for criticism of the private sector where called for and for advocacy of the private sector and the strengthening of this vital element in our national tradition of pluralism. This is, quite obviously, not an easy prescription to fulfill.

The British Model

The notion of establishing some new body to aid, or perhaps oversee, the third sector is not new. Indeed, a number of proposals in this regard have been advanced in recent years. They have ranged from relatively modest ones—the creation of what would be essentially an information clearinghouse—to recommendations for establishing new regulatory agencies with wide-ranging authority and judicial powers. The latter generally take their inspiration, at least in part, from the Charity Commission in Britain, which traces its origins back to 1601 and which now has a staff of 360 with broad powers to oversee that country's 115,000 "charitable" organizations.

By contrast, whatever governmental authority is exercised in this area in the United States is widely dispersed. It resides for the most part in the courts, in state attorneys general and in the Internal Revenue Service. The last is the nation's single most influential overseer of the philanthropic world, because of its power to determine, within broad limits of the law, what organizations are eligible for charitable status and therefore can receive tax-deductible gifts. Yet the IRS's oversight is incidental to its revenue-collecting role.

After considering various existing and proposed alternatives, the Commission feels that a regulatory agency with full governmental status and wide authority, modeled on the British Charity Commission, is not transplantable into the American context and that the present pattern of enforcement and oversight of nonprofit organizations should, with the changes proposed in the previous chapter, be maintained.

Quasi-Governmental Status

Yet the Commission does feel that there is indeed a need for an organization with analysis and advancement of the nonprofit sector as a central purpose. And while rejecting proposals that such an organization be a governmental agency, like the Charity Commission, we do see considerable merit in quasi-governmental status for any national oganization on the nonprofit sector.

Government and the nonprofit sector are obviously and undeniably related in their public purposes, they are linked through the tax system and there is a wide intermix of public and private support for public and private organizations. We hope and believe that a commission with governmental input would act as a catalyst to bring together the two sectors in more deliberate ways so that they will work more fruitfully together, and more harmoniously than they have at times. The relative virtues of one sector in comparison with the other are best exercised, we believe, not in competition but in co-alignment. As a glance at the social agenda, the catalogue of unfilled public needs, of this country indicates, there is more than enough for both sectors to do. The expectation that they will share the burdens more productively underlies our proposal for a commisson that will embody among its underlying rationales, a conscious, structural linking of the two sectors on the basis of a clearer definition of their respective roles, responsibilities, capabilities and limitations.

Recommendation

To give concreteness to this concept as a basis for public discussion, the Commission accordingly, in terminating its own work, puts forward as one of its major recommendations:

*That a permanent national commission on the nonprofit sector be established by Congress.**

This permanent commission should work closely and continuously with both the legislative and executive branches of government, as well as with the private sector, but it should remain one degree removed from both purely private and fully official status.

The following is an outline of the proposed purposes and structure of such a commission on the private nonprofit sector:

PURPOSES

1. To construct and disseminate for public enlightenment and use as complete a data base as possible on the present sources and uses of the resources of the private nonprofit sector. In this connection the commission might establish a registry of private voluntary organizations.

2. To observe trends and periodically update existing data, so that the new commission can stand ready to speak authoritatively on the existing state and the future needs of the pri-

*See dissents by GEORGE ROMNEY, page 221, and by RAYMOND J. GALLAGHER, page 222.

vate sector. To aid in this role, it is envisioned that the commission would have full access to pertinent IRS data within limits set by the rights of privacy.

3. To explore and suggest ways of strengthening the role of private philanthropy and the entire private nonprofit sector in our society, not only in terms of increased financial support and volunteered services but also of enhanced public knowledge and appreciation of that role.

4. To provide a forum for public discussion of issues affecting the nonprofit sector and for commentary, critical or otherwise, directed toward the sector.

5. To study in depth the existing relationships between government and the nonprofit sector; to seek ways of encouraging and improving existing relationships in a spirit of cooperation while preserving the effectiveness and independence of the sector and the private initiative which gives it life; and to serve actively in close consultation with government as an ombudsman in the protection of the interests of the private nonprofit sector.

FORMATION

By Act of Congress.

MEMBERS

Broad public membership is essential, and so a total commission membership of 20 to 25 individuals is proposed. Ex-officio and other special representation memberships should be avoided in favor of selection on the basis of experience and genuine interest and concern for the areas of the commission's work.*

The initial membership might be chosen as follows, assuming a total of 25 members:

1. The President selects the commission's chairman.

2. The President (presumably working with the chairman) names 12 other members.

3. All Presidential appointees are subject to senatorial confirmation.

4. The 13 members so named then select the remaining 12 members.

*See comment by MAX M. FISHER, page 222.

The term of membership in the commission should be three to five years. No member should be able to serve for more than two successive terms.

FUNDING

The commission's budget should be met from government appropriations and from private sources, ideally one half from each. A ceiling should be placed on individual private contributions, so that private funding comes from many sources. A modest charge on all charitable organizations should be considered, or possibly the new audit fee that the Commission proposes for foundations could be enlarged to provide funds specifically earmarked for the new commission.

TERM OF EXISTENCE

The commission should be granted permanent status, subject of course to periodic review and, ultimately, the commission's own demonstration of its benefit to the society.

Sources for Chapter VIII

Arthur Andersen & Co., *Overview of Governmental Support and Financial Regulation of Philanthropic Organizations in Selected Nations.**

Thomas R. Asher, *Public Needs, Public Policy and Philanthropy.**

Robert J. Blendon, *The Changing Role of Private Philanthropy in Health Affairs.**

Gerard M. Brannon and James Strnad, *Alternative Approaches to Encouraging Philanthropic Activities.**

Robert H. Bremner, *Private Philanthropy and Public Needs: An Historical Perspective.**

John J. Carson and Harry V. Hodson, eds., *Philanthropy in the '70's: An Anglo-American Discussion,* Council on Foundations, Inc., New York, 1973.

David Ginsburg, Lee R. Marks and Ronald P. Wertheim, *Federal Oversight of Private Philanthropy.**

Eric Larrabee, *The Public Funding Agency.**

Reynold Levy and Waldemar A. Nielsen, *An Agenda for the Future.**

Peter G. Meek, *Self-Regulation in Private Philanthropy.**

Donald R. Spuehler, *The System for Regulation and Assistance of Charity in England and Wales with Recommendations as to Establishment of a National Commission on Philanthropy in the United States.**

Adam Yarmolinsky and Marion R. Fremont-Smith, *Preserving the Private Voluntary Sector: A Proposal for a Public Advisory Commission on Philanthropy.**

*Denotes reports and studies undertaken for the Commission.

COMMENTS
and
DISSENTS

COMMENTS AND DISSENTS

Page 33, by GRACIELA OLIVAREZ

The Commission on Private Philanthropy and Public Needs was charged over two years ago with an important national mission: to review the direction and status of charitable giving in this country and to assess its ability to meet public needs. Perhaps the great weakness in the Commission's report is that no definition of public need was ever offered. Granted, public need is open to competing definitions. But the fact that the Commission chose to defer this fundamental responsibility is indicative of the general tenor of its conclusions and recommendations, which avoid issues that are controversial and complex and in essence support maintenance of the status quo. I believe that ample modifications in the present system of charitable giving are essential if philanthropy is to be a viable alternative to government and is to meet real public need. Yet the net result of the Commission's two years of study, aside from a necessary and relatively strong statement of support for the voluntary sector's legal freedom to attempt to influence legislation, has been to give little more than verbal tokenism to the need for change in the current philanthropic structure.

Page 69, by FRANCES T. FARENTHOLD, GRACIELA OLIVAREZ and ALTHEA T. L. SIMMONS

The Commission on Private Philanthropy and Public Needs is itself a prime example of institutional philanthropy's neglect of women and women's interests. While women constitute 53 per cent of the American population, only four out of 28 Commission members have been women and only eight out of the Commission's 118 advisors have been women. No study was prepared on women—on either the role of women in nonprofit organizations and philanthropy or the role of nonprofit organizations and philanthropy in furthering—or failing to further—the aspirations, needs and rights of women. Other than at this particular part of its report, the Commission's findings and recommendations hardly mention women or the women's movement.

197

This disregard of women is symptomatic of a larger short-coming of the Commission: its refusal to recognize that philan-thropy as presently constituted has by and large failed to meet the needs of important new, or newly striving, groups in the society. An even larger shortcoming that underlies the Com-mission's neglect of women has been the Commission's failure to reexamine philanthropy and the use of philanthropic re-sources in light of the immense social changes that have taken place in the last decade.

Women and the needs of women do not constitute the only such area of social change that the Commission's examination of philanthropy has failed to take into account; the Commis-sion has virtually failed to heed any such changes in what has been an obvious predisposition to defend the status quo both in the institutions that encourage or dispense philanthropic giving in the United States and in the institutions that benefit from such giving.

Yet the meager representation of women on or around the Commission and the Commission's virtual silence on women in its research, its deliberations, its findings and its recommenda-tions all provide some of the more glaring evidences of the Commission's narrow range of vision. That this narrowness has severely limited the usefulness of the Commission's examina-tion of philanthropy and the nonprofit sector is amply illustrat-ed by what the Commission did *not* find out about women in relation to these areas.

The Commission failed to recognize that the concerns of women are an integral part of the solution to every major social problem.

- The problems of population growth cannot be addressed without reference to the economic and social status of women and the myths they are forced to live out.
- The problems of ecology and natural resources cannot be addressed without consideration of the role of women as consumers and mothers.
- The problems of poverty cannot be addressed without rec-ognition of the fact that being poor is directly correlated with being female.
- The problems of the delivery of health care and prevention cannot be addressed without reference to women as con-

198

sumers and providers of health services.

- The problems of mental health cannot be addressed without consideration of the destructive impact of sex discrimination on the personalities of women and men.

The Commission failed to recognize ways in which traditional recipients of philanthropy contribute to the discrimination against women. In higher education, to take a major recipient area:

- Women are discriminated against on faculties, as evidenced by wide salary gaps between men and women, and by the fact that in 1974, 57 per cent of male faculty members were granted tenure, while only 26.7 per cent of women faculty members were granted tenure.
- The unemployment rates among professionals are two to three times higher for women than for men.
- The percentage of women graduate and undergraduate students is lower than in 1930.
- Many women are part-time students, which makes them ineligible for almost every form of fellowship and grant aid available. Many who postpone their education during a period of childrearing are also eliminated by age restrictions.
- The median education level of black women has risen only two thirds as much as that for black men between 1966 and 1972.
- Illogical clumping of women in only a few areas of study occurs.
- Though women complete bachelor's degrees faster and with substantially higher grades than men, women are less likely to go on to graduate school.

An analysis of other nonprofit organizations and institutions would have documented further a generally shameful record throughout the nonprofit sector in connection with the status of women. To cite only two elements in this record:

- Women rarely appear, in more than token numbers, on professional staffs or the boards of foundations and churches.
- The United Way gives boys' organizations four dollars to every one dollar that goes to girls' organizations.

The Commission failed to identify women as a major section of the powerless.

A paper prepared for the Commission, entitled "Philanthropy and the Powerless," omitted women entirely. That women must be identified among the powerless is unquestionable considering the economic disadvantages of women, the systemic barriers to political participation by women, the cultural handicaps imposed upon women, and the over-repression inflicted upon certain portions of the female population.

- Women hold only 4 to 7 per cent of all public offices in this nation.
- Between 1960 and 1967 the number of forcible rapes upon women increased by 61 per cent. But the proportion followed by arrest decreased annually. The FBI shows that 86 per cent of aggravated assault cases were solved, as compared to only 5 per cent of rape cases.

Another important area in which the Commission has failed to look at women and women's relationship to philanthropy and nonprofit activity—and thereby further evidences its failure to take account of social change—is in the area of volunteerism. Significantly more women than men serve as volunteers—one out of four women do some volunteer work while only one out of five men do. Yet it is clear that the women volunteer force that serves as a basic resource for many nonprofit groups and agencies can no longer be taken for granted in the economics of philanthropy. One reason, probably the main reason, that more women than men have traditionally served as volunteers is that fewer women have held regular jobs. Yet, as women are joining the labor force in ever increasing proportions, it is almost certain that women in general will be contributing fewer hours of volunteer work. The implications of this change must be profound for philanthropy, but the Commission has not considered this area of change at all.

Again, while we speak as women with particular concern about the Commission's failure to examine—let alone propose remedies for—the nonprofit sector's severe shortcomings in dealing with the aspirations and needs of women, we emphasize that we see this failure as part of a broader failure. This is the Commission's unwillingness to examine in any profound and penetrating way the existing role of philanthropy and nonprofit activity and to propose new roles, with new structures

and new incentives, that are appropriate to the rapidly changing world of the mid-1970's.

At its best, private philanthropy can play a significant role
in alleviating the maldistribution of power and wealth in
American society. It has the freedom and flexibility to support
those endeavors which truly are on the cutting edge of social
change. But this is true only if it is willing to listen to the
advocates of social change, that is those who are articulating
public needs as seen from the point of view of those in need.

So long as public needs are defined by the philanthropists
rather than by the recipients, by the "haves" rather than the
"have nots," philanthropy will simply serve the interests of the
former to the neglect of the latter. The Commission has completely failed to appreciate this fact. It has by-passed the question of defining public needs as being too difficult, and come
down on the side of preserving the status quo in philanthropy:
support for health facilities, private higher education and the
arts. The Commission has failed to understand that this in and
of itself amounts to a de facto definition of public needs. To
those groups in American society which are clamoring for their
fair share of the resources and power in the richest and most
democratic nation the world has ever known, such a definition
is totally unacceptable.

Page 123, by MAX M. FISHER, with which LESTER CROWN,
RAYMOND J. GALLAGHER, PHILIP M. KLUTZNICK and
RALPH LAZARUS have asked to be associated

The writing of the text of the report does not do justice to
the substance of the Commission's discussions, nor to its conclusions. This point was made in the Commission's own discussions of preliminary drafts.

The report is excessively a defensive response to a series of
alleged criticisms of philanthropy. A number of the sections
begin with negative attacks or criticisms of current elements of
philanthropy, and then respond to them. This format does a
disservice to philanthropy and to the Commission's own pos-
ture, and to the impact of its recommendations.

The significance of the Commission's work should not be
measured by the extent to which its findings may or may not

201

differ from current provisions. The test rather should be whether the Commission has followed a careful searching process in which all alternatives were examined as a pre-condition for determining whether current provisions should be retained or new provisions should be recommended. That test has been met in large measure.

Another defect in the report is the distortion of the concepts of "equity" and "democracy" applied to philanthropic giving by the wealthy. The fact that the wealthy make the largest gifts, and have the freedom to decide the objects of their gifts, is referred to as inequitable and undemocratic. Yet it is the essence of equity and democracy for people who have the largest means to make the largest philanthropic contributions. It is also the essence of democracy and pluralism, and the strength of voluntary philanthropy, that givers should be able to designate the purposes and the objects of their gifts.

The comments refer specifically to the fact that there is a 70 per cent deduction for gifts of persons who are in the 70 per cent bracket of tax payments. Since the two provisions are directly linked, that must be recognized as a balancing factor, and not an inequity.

Charitable gifts do not benefit the wealthy. They benefit the human needs financed by the gifts. The wealthy would benefit if they did not make the gifts; the gift is a 100 per cent tax, and the contributor retains none of it; if he chose not to give, and were in the 70 per cent bracket, he would retain 30 per cent for his own use.

Page 127, by MAX M. FISHER, with which LESTER CROWN, RAYMOND J. GALLAGHER, PHILIP M. KLUTZNICK AND RALPH LAZARUS have asked to be associated

Reference is made to guidance of gifts to particular purposes. It is essential in voluntary philanthropy, as in America generally, that recognition be given to the indispensability of many values held by many different people. Who is to say which value is "right" and which value is "wrong"? Who is to say which value is more important than others? Who is to deny that relative values with relative importance change over periods of time? There should be no imposition or attempted imposition of monolithic values.

Page 133, by MAX M. FISHER, with which LESTER CROWN, BAYARD EWING, RAYMOND J. GALLAGHER, PHILIP M. KLUTZNICK and RALPH LAZARUS have asked to be associated

Reference is made to the preferences of upper-income givers in the selection of the objects of donations. This distorts the element of choice, which is exercised by all givers. Other sections of the Commission's report point out that the persons with middle-level income provide the greatest combined total of philanthropy; their selection of donees is proportionately great.

There is the added reality, omitted by the Commission's report, that patterns of support reflect what *donees seek*, as well as what donors select. Churches do not seek large individual gifts as a pattern, especially for their operating purposes. Universities do seek very large individual gifts, not only for current operations, but for capital and endowment purposes. Donee influence likewise affects bequests. It is too simplistic to attribute the patterns of objects of gifts only to the wishes of the donors.

Page 135, by ELIZABETH J. McCORMACK, with which EDWIN D. ETHERINGTON, FRANCES T. FARENTHOLD, EARL G. GRAVES, WILLIAM M. ROTH and LEON H. SULLIVAN have asked to be associated

While we agree unequivocally that greater tax incentives for giving should be instituted for low- and middle-income taxpayers to build a broad democratic base for the nonprofit sector, we disagree that the "double deduction" is the best means to this end for two reasons:
1. Within the range of its application, a 200 per cent "double deduction" for giving, or any similar variation of the regular charitable deduction, intensifies the very shortcoming it is supposed to remedy. The principal reason for moving beyond the charitable deduction as an incentive for giving is to correct a perceived inequity or imbalance

in the deduction itself—the fact that because of its relationship to the progressive income tax the deduction provides a greater tax savings for giving the higher the giver's income level.

A "double deduction" for taxpayers with incomes under $15,000, and a deduction of 150 per cent for those with incomes between $15,000 and $30,000, would not only fail to correct this imbalance, it would exaggerate it throughout an income range within which most taypayers fall. Taxpayers at the minimum 14 per cent marginal tax rate level would save 28 cents for each dollar given, while taxpayers at the 32 per cent marginal rate would save 48 cents. It is hard to see how equity would be served rather than further offended by such a formula.

The only way to remedy the amplified inequity of an amplified deduction would be to structure the deduction so that it went up in steps as the income of the deductor went down. But any such gradation would be extremely complicated for the taxpayer to understand and use and would ultimately amount to a very convoluted way of arriving at the same end served by a tax credit, that is, providing the same proportionate level of tax savings to all contributors regardless of their income.

2. The simplicity of the tax law is essential to the taxpayer's understanding of what is justly due him. The "double deduction", we maintain, is too complex to be easily understood by the average individual without ready access to an attorney or accountant. Without such assistance, the taxpayer is unlikely to know the real cost of giving. What is not understood, we believe, will not be used.

Page 135, by GRACIELA OLIVAREZ

The Commission recommends that greater equity in giving be achieved by permitting individuals who use the standard deduction to deduct charitable giving as well. I feel this kind of measure will create little to no incentive to give for people in middle to low income brackets because of the essentially regressive nature of the deduction. Indeed, even the Commission gave tacit recognition to this conclusion when it considered a

204

proposal that persons earning $30,000 or less be given a ten per cent tax credit for charitable giving. Unfortunately, this proposal for a credit was overturned in favor of supporting maintenance of the present regressive system of giving incentives, thus denying to a large sector of society the opportunity to take advantage of an equitable and realistic tax incentive. The inequity of the charitable deduction is also acknowledged implicitly by the Commission's additional recommendation for deductions of 200 or 150 per cent of giving. But this proposal appears to have little virtue other than keeping faith with the deduction. It still leaves the middle and low income giver with a much lower incentive to give than the wealthy giver. In fact, among those it would apply to, it actually widens the disparity of incentives. As usual, philanthropy is treated as if it were principally the domain of the wealthy and near wealthy, and little effort has been made to truly broaden the base of philanthropy.

Page 135, by ALAN PIFER, with which LESTER CROWN, BAYARD EWING, PHILIP M. KLUTZNICK and JOHN M. MUSSER have asked to be associated

Since $15,000 is now only slightly above the median family income for the nation, there would be a rough sort of equity involved in allowing a double deduction for gifts to charity for families with incomes below that amount. I therefore support this part of the recommendation. The Commission's proposal, however, for a 150 per cent deduction for gifts by families in the $15,000-$30,000 range, despite its probable efficiency in stimulating substantial new giving, has the serious fault of simply increasing the inequitable aspects of the present deduction system. I, therefore, dissociate myself from this part of the recommendation.

Page 139, by ELIZABETH J. McCORMACK, with which EDWIN D. ETHERINGTON, FRANCES T. FARENTHOLD, WILLIAM M. ROTH and LEON H. SULLIVAN have asked to be associated

Two objectives of the Commission have been to achieve greater equity and to broaden the base of philanthropy.

We believe that a forceful step is needed to redress the inequity that results from the incentive for charitable giving based on the progressive income tax. In effect, it costs the high-income taxpayer far less to give a dollar to charity than it does the poor man. We believe further that it is of the highest importance to encourage in all individuals a sense of responsibility for general welfare through the practice of philanthropic giving. In the long run the vitality of the nonprofit sector will depend on this broadly based support.

We therefore recommend a simple tax credit of $50 to $100 for all individuals with incomes of up to $10,000.

The tax credit allows a giver to subtract the amount of the credit, dollar for dollar, from taxes owed. The relationship between giving and taxes is clear and direct and would therefore appear to be a more effective incentive to giving. Only experience will give a firm answer to the question of the "efficiency" of the tax credit, but in our opinion more new giving will be stimulated than is predicted.

We believe that money made available to the individual through this tax credit should be viewed not as money withheld from government but rather as funds that the government requires be earmarked for causes and organizations in the public interest and of the individual's own choosing. This process can be looked upon as a continuous referendum in which the voting is done not through the electoral mechanism but through tax-creditable giving.

In other words, the broader view is advocated here that tax obligations are not obligations to support the costs of government per se but to support public purposes, the large proportion of which are selected and financed through governmental programs. But under a charitable credit a significant portion would be selected by individuals. Individual allocation of a share of tax money to public purposes should, we propose, become established as an important right of citizenship and an underpinning of our pluralistic society. We should not be timid or apprehensive about accepting a charitable tax credit in this positive light.

206

Page 140, by MAX M. FISHER, with which LESTER CROWN, RAYMOND J. GALLAGHER, PHILIP M. KLUTZNICK and RALPH LAZARUS have asked to be associated

Tax credits are regarded as based on an erroneous premise that charitable gifts are government funds; rather, they are the donations of private funds by citizens. Furthermore, tax credits raise constitutional questions if provided for church purposes. And by endangering the size of the largest gifts, the leadership donations which also attract other gifts, the effect of tax credits could be a harmful reduction in contributions.

Page 143, by ELIZABETH J. McCORMACK, with which EDWIN D. ETHERINGTON, BAYARD EWING, FRANCES T. FARENTHOLD, EARL G. GRAVES, WALTER A. HAAS, JR., GRACIELA OLIVAREZ, ALAN PIFER, WILLIAM M. ROTH and LEON H. SULLIVAN have asked to be associated

We unequivocally recommend a minimum income tax. We believe that income devoted to charitable giving should be made subject to any minimum income tax law. All who are financially able have an obligation to support the costs of government. As worthy as nonprofit causes may be, it should not be possible for any individual to have, in effect, the option of financially supporting such causes instead of paying any taxes. Yet such an option remains if charitable giving is not included in determining what income a minimum tax is to be based upon.

We see the inclusion of charitable giving in a minimum income tax as not only reflecting a basic obligation of citizenship but as an important safeguard and benefit to the nonprofit sector itself. The major argument for the exclusion of charitable contributions from the minimum tax is that such a change would greatly discourage giving. Yet indications are that the amount of possible loss to the nonprofit sector would in fact be relatively small. The weighing of minimum tax effects in such terms seems to us to be dangerously shortsighted; it overlooks the potentially far more serious cost to charity of undermining the legitimacy of the income tax system itself.

The charitable deduction and the giving it stimulates clearly

207

depend on the effective functioning of the income tax system, which depends in turn on a high degree of public confidence that the system works equitably. Yet the possibility that some can avoid paying taxes, when tax-deductible giving is coupled with other deductions, must bring the tax system profoundly into question in the eyes of the great majority who neither have nor presumably would exercise such an option. We believe, therefore, that nonprofit organizations have more to gain from the elimination of such a possibility than from its continuation.

Page 143, by MAX M. FISHER, with which LESTER CROWN, RAYMOND J. GALLAGHER, PHILIP M. KLUTZNICK and RALPH LAZARUS have asked to be associated

The section on gifts of appreciated property does not do justice to the Commission's convictions and conclusions on the vital importance of such gifts. This difference between the negative approach of the text of the report and the Commission's recommendations was discussed by the Commission, in reacting to the first draft, but the changes in the writing which were called for have not been made. Thus, the setting for the treatment of this subject in pages 143-145, opening the consideration with a series of attacks, sets the discussion in a negative framework which is neither objective nor factual. The anti-large giver bias is particularly striking.

Donors of appreciated property do not benefit financially from their gifts. The 1969 tax laws made such a possiblity extremely rare. The beneficiaries are the people and needs receiving the gifts.

"The appreciated property tax allowances provide added inducements to give that are not related to the value of the gift to the charitable recipient." No basis is given for that statement. The contrary is true: charities generally record the market value of the gift on the day it is received.

The point is made ". . . people with the same income and giving are treated differently, depending upon whether one gives cash and the other property." This implies favoritism to the donor of property. It ignores that there is a 50 per cent limit applying to cash gifts, whereas there is a 30 per cent limit applying to gifts of appreciated property.

The statement is made ". . . the size of the tax inducement does not correspond to the size of the benefit obtained by the charitable recipient or society as a whole." That statement is incomprehensible. No explanation is given, nor any facts to substantiate it.

It should be clear that criticisms of deductions of appreciated property are not synonymous with tax reform, and that not all tax reform advocates by any means share the criticisms of the deduction of appreciated property.

The statement is made ". . . many Commission members agree that the appreciated property provision in the charitable deduction, when looked at by itself, challenges standards of both tax principle and social equity . . ." This does not, it should be emphasized, represent the view of the full Commission. Its discussions revealed strong contrary views. Social equity must take into account the benefits to society from these gifts, the losses there would be to the beneficiaries if such gifts were not made, and that the beneficiaries are not the wealthy.

Page 146, by BAYARD EWING

A specific example of the effect of eliminating the appreciated property allowance can be seen in the tax provision limiting practicing artists to a deduction equal to the cost of materials contained in works of their own manufacture when such works are donated to museums. This provision has resulted in a complete drying up of such gifts with no counter-balancing increase in gifts of cash.

Page 147, by GRACIELA OLIVAREZ

The issue of appreciated property is highly controversial, as debate among commissioners has shown. The recommendation offered by the Commission is only partially satisfactory. It does permit maximization of the charitable dollar and proposes to bar personal financial gain through tax-deductible charitable giving. This would be acceptable only as long as donors of appreciated property are bound to pay a minimal income tax.

Page 151, by GRACIELA OLIVAREZ

I do not completely agree with the majority recommendation that the charitable bequest deduction be retained in its current form. The bequest deduction cannot be viewed in isolation. It is inextricably linked to more profound principles of taxation and should be studied in such context. Furthermore, I feel strongly that a minimal tax be applied to the bequest—in the spirit of principle which underlies my firm support of minimum income and appreciated property taxation.

Page 157, by FRANCES T. FARENTHOLD, with which BAYARD EWING has asked to be associated

Employing exhortation to increase corporate gifts to charity is a futile exercise. Most of the corporate members of the Commission acknowledged in our meetings that mere talk had not and would not increase corporate contributions.

We therefore support a proposal which would impose a 2 per cent needs tax on corporate income. The tax could be offset either partially or completely by cash gifts to charity.

This proposal would guarantee an increase in corporate giving. It would have the further advantage that public utilities (some of whom are not permitted by regulators to make contributions) and corporations under negative pressure from stockholders would relieve themselves from all objections to contributing by this measure.

Page 157, by GRACIELA OLIVAREZ

Corporate giving was perhaps the one area which revealed the least amount of consent among the commissioners. This appears evident from the inconclusive recommendation that further study be given the issue. But the Commission has had two years to assess corporate giving. I believe that corporations should be subject to a surtax not to exceed 2 per cent of income. Any difference between the 2 per cent and the proportion of income contributed to charity would be added to taxable income. This proviso would be applied to companies accumulating incomes of $500,000 or more.

Page 157, by WILLIAM M. ROTH, with which LESTER CROWN, ELIZABETH J. McCORMACK and WALTER A. HAAS, JR. have asked to be associated

It is obvious from the record that exhortation has not worked to increase corporate giving, and there is no evidence that exhortation will work any better between now and 1980 than it has in the past. Accordingly, it is necessary to resort to other measures if there is to be any real hope that corporate giving will rise above the current average of about 1 per cent of pre-tax net income, most of which is given by a few corporations.

We would favor the adoption of a 1 per cent or 2 per cent "vanishing floor" for corporate giving, requiring corporations to give at least 1 per cent or 2 per cent of annual pre-tax net income in order to qualify for the charitable deduction. If the floor were met, all giving would be deductible up to the 5 per cent limit set by law; if not, none of the giving would be deductible.

Because of expressed concerns that the "vanishing floor" might retard giving rather than enhance it, the provision should be adopted on a trial basis for three to five years. If giving did not increase, other measures, such as the "philanthropic tax" mentioned in the report, should then be considered.

Page 160, by MAX M. FISHER, with which LESTER CROWN, BAYARD EWING, RAYMOND J. GALLAGHER, PHILIP M. KLUTZNICK and RALPH LAZARUS have asked to be associated

The statements on these pages are erroneous. The nonprofit agencies *are* in the market place of competition for philanthropic dollars. Givers have a number of choices for their contributions. Middle-income and wealthy givers are solicited for many contributions each year. They have many choices to make in giving or withholding contributions.

The fact is that nonprofit agencies not only must attract gifts in competition with others, but they must justify the continuation of support, year after year.

Reference is made to the public "skepticism" and "cynicism," without supporting, solid facts that this characterization is accurate regarding philanthropy. The support of philanthropy indicates the opposite.

Page 161, by MAX M. FISHER, with which LESTER CROWN, RAYMOND J. GALLAGHER, PHILIP M. KLUTZNICK and RALPH LAZARUS have asked to be associated

In presenting the need for the free flow of information between voluntary groups and the public-at-large, recognition must be given to the fact that many nonprofit agencies are single purpose organizations and appeal to persons committed to that purpose. The treatment of this whole section should take due account of that fact, rather than expecting all organizations to deal with the entire public.

Page 161, by MAX M. FISHER, with which LESTER CROWN, RAYMOND J. GALLAGHER, PHILIP M. KLUTZNICK and RALPH LAZARUS have asked to be associated

The reference to meetings and reports of donee organizations as "operating imperfectly at best" fails to take account of the fact that many of the organizations, and especially the largest ones spending the greatest funds, do issue commendable reports.

Page 163, by MAX M. FISHER, with which LESTER CROWN, RAYMOND J. GALLAGHER, PHILIP M. KLUTZNICK and RALPH LAZARUS have asked to be associated

The report refers to the "loose and even haphazard procedures that some nonprofit organizations employ to make themselves accountable to the public." That is entirely too sweeping a statement. It ignores current reporting requirements of federal and state governments and the existence of contributor information services in many localities.

Page 163, by MAX M. FISHER, with which LESTER CROWN, BAYARD EWING, RAYMOND J. GALLAGHER, PHILIP M. KLUTZNICK and RALPH LAZARUS have asked to be associated

No facts are cited in the report to substantiate the individ-

212

ual's opinion, referring to nonprofit agencies as a "private club." It is extremely destructive. Without a body of facts to underpin any such criticism, it is far too sweeping for the Commission to quote with any implication of credibility.

Page 164, by ELIZABETH J. McCORMACK, with which EDWIN D. ETHERINGTON, BAYARD EWING, FRANCES T. FARENTHOLD, EARL G. GRAVES, WALTER A. HAAS, JR., JOHN M. MUSSER, ALAN PIFER, WILLIAM M. ROTH and LEON H. SULLIVAN have asked to be associated

Except for their purely sacramental activities, religious organizations should not be excluded from the disclosure requirements that the Commission has recommended for other tax-exempt charitable organizations. In many cases, religious affiliates are barely distinguishable from secular organizations in the functions they perform, for example, in the fields of education and health. It is therefore entirely appropriate, we hold, that these organizations carrying out nonsacramental activities be held to the same standards of public accountability as other tax-exempt institutions.

Page 166, by MAX M. FISHER, with which LESTER CROWN, BAYARD EWING, RAYMOND J. GALLAGHER, PHILIP M. KLUTZNICK and RALPH LAZARUS have asked to be associated

The point is properly made that there should be more uniformity in accounting and reporting by *comparable* organizations. That is already more of a fact than the report indicates. For example, it is true among hospitals and among universities which spend very substantial philanthropic funds, and among other types of philanthropic organizations. The United Way has issued guides for uniform accounting and reporting by welfare organizations. The Assembly of National Voluntary Health and Social Welfare Organizations several years ago developed uniform standards—and there are other examples. Further progress is dependent on the readiness of the AICPA and the FASB to move ahead—not alone on the agencies which have heretofore taken the initiative.

213

Page 166, by ALAN PIFER, with which LESTER CROWN, EDWIN D. ETHERINGTON and JOHN M. MUSSER have asked to be associated

Replacement of the tax on foundations by a smaller audit fee would, of course, be preferable to retention of the tax in its present form and at its current 4 per cent level. Nonetheless, this recommendation, if adopted, would not remove the underlying objection to any special levy on foundations whatsoever. These objections are:

1. That such a levy deprives charitable recipients of resources at a time when such resources are needed as never before;
2. That a tax on charity is contradictory in principle, in that public authority, whose responsibility it is to promote the general welfare, is thereby denying funds to entities which exist for no other purpose; and
3. That, since auditing is a normal function of government, there is no logical reason why any particular class of organizations should have to pay for the privilege of being audited.

In short, any levy on foundations, whatever its level and whatever it is called, is philosophically wrong and basically discriminatory.

Page 167, by GRACIELA OLIVAREZ

I maintain that the regulatory functions of the IRS should be transferred to another agency, specifically the proposed commission on the nonprofit sector. Recent questionable activities of the the IRS alone make that agency suspect. Apart from that, however, placing charitable activities under the scrutiny of IRS seems to be a tradition rooted in the wisdom that any sector accorded special tax status automatically be regulated by the central tax authority. Philanthropy, I maintain, is a far broader concept and practice than 501(c)(3), and should fall within the regulatory purview of a special entity created for and sensitive to that purpose.

Page 167, by FRANCES T. FARENTHOLD

The Commission's report has no greater blind spot than its refusal to acknowledge the recent revelations of past and continuing perversions of government agencies for political purposes. The unprecedented abuses of power still being exposed in the wake of the Watergate phenomenon make it clear that the Internal Revenue Service should not be the agency regulating exempt organizations.

These revelations have shown that the IRS has systematically established procedures, under the last five presidents at least, to subject politically unfavored exempt organizations to denial of exemption, excessive delay in rulings on exempt status and audit procedures extraordinary in both frequency and intensity. Contrary to the Commission's assertion that "except in several isolated instances, the Service has demonstrated its capacity for independent, impartial oversight of tax exempt organizations," the IRS:

1. During the McCarthy era, under both Truman and Eisenhower administrations, denied and revoked exemptions of "subversive" organizations.

2. During the Kennedy and Johnson administrations established an "ideological organization project" which disrupted the activities of those exempt groups that were viewed as threats from the right or left.

3. During the Nixon administration established a "Special Service Staff" to harrass left-wing tax-exempt organizations.

Even without their continuing history of politicization of the regulation of exempt organizations, most observers agree with Alan Pifer. He said that present regulation is "quite ineffective, it is characterized by a negative rather than a positive attitude toward charity and it is located in the wrong place within the government."

The Commission's own study in this area says that the officials who are responsible for regulating exempt organizations are "handicapped by (a) cumbersome procedures which were designed generally to meet the needs of the tax- collecting branches of the Service; (b) inadequate authority in relation to other officials near the top of the Service's hierarchy; (c) the understandable emphasis of the Service on its role as tax collector rather than as overseer of a non-revenue producing activity; and (d) the generally weaker qualifications and training

215

of the Service's field staff as compared to the National Office staff."

All of this leads to conclude that all ruling and audit functions regarding exempt organizations should be removed from IRS and placed in a new independent regulatory commission.

This new commission would also have greater credibility and more potential for performing the research and advocacy function envisioned by the Commission report for the proposed permanent national commission on philanthropy.

Page 168, by FRANCES T. FARENTHOLD

The Commission has not addressed the problems of one of the most important developments in the past 25 years, the rise and proliferation of federated fund-raising campaigns. The phenomenon of the United Way arose from the desire of corporate management to control the solicitation and disbursement of charitable funds and through that process to control the operation of social service agencies in their communities.

Because United Ways were created to meet the needs of donors rather than either the needs of the organizational recipients or of the public, many problems of fund-raising ethics, governance, accessibility, allocation and accountability have arisen.

One of the most important issues is the system of payroll deduction which in many instances, as one observer put it, "approaches taxation in its mechanical and, not always subtle, coercive technique of raising and allocating funds." This system enables the businessmen who control the United Way boards to increase the disparity between classes in giving as a percentage of income. The corporations and their officers consistently give a smaller percentage of income than do low-income workers.

The corporations not only exert pressure on their workers to give to the United Ways and substitute for their own giving but they allow the United Ways a complete monopoly of the payroll deduction process. This, combined with the domination of United Way boards by the businessmen, denies the worker effective control over whether he gives, to whom he gives and to what use his "gift" is put.

216

This domination of the United Way allocation committees by corporate officers and their favorite charities insures that the allocation patterns of the past remain the same. Access of new agencies representing changing needs is consistently denied. For instance, one recent study shows an average change of only 0.56 per cent in United Way allocations nationally.

Even with all of these faults, the United Way could function as a valuable tool for social change on the local level. A source of funds for such a purpose is so sorely needed now that large amounts of funds and power are shifting from the federal government to states and cities without any accompanying reform of local government.

This Commission has denied sufficient space to suggest specific remedies to these many problems but I felt it imperative to at least insert this note for the public's attention.

Page 168, by MAX M. FISHER, with which LESTER CROWN, BAYARD EWING, RAYMOND J. GALLAGHER, PHILIP M. KLUTZNICK and RALPH LAZARUS have asked to be associated

The report distorts the situation by attributing to public charities situations that involve some foundations.

Especially singled out by the report among the public charities are federated fund-raising organizations. Yet they are the most public of the public charities and often the most accessible, involving the broadest cross sections of all major elements of communities, including racial and ethnic minorities.

No facts are cited to support the allegations of "closed doors and closed minds." It is altogether too sweeping and inaccurate.

Page 170, by FRANCES T. FARENTHOLD

The Commission's exhortation to nonprofit organizations to broaden the composition and viewpoints of their boards and staffs won't have great impact on that large group of grant-making organizations which have no staff. The lack of staff is, in some instances, as great an impediment to accessibility as the insularity of governing boards. There can be no real consideration of proposals, much less affirmative outreach, unless there is adequate staff.

The Commission has not even gone as far as the Peterson Commission did in 1970. They urged foundations to hire staff themselves or "to consider merging into existing community foundations" or "to pool their resources to share the services of a professional administrator" or to "form associations of foundations interested in a similar program area and jointly hire an expert."

The report of the Council on Foundations to this Commission indicates that there are indeed more foundation staff now than before the 1969 Tax Reform Act and the Peterson report. But the survey also demonstrates that, for the most part, staff were hired to deal with the administrative complexities of that act rather than to enhance the foundations' program functions.

By all accounts, the vast majority of foundations have no professional staff and of all reported staff, 23 per cent work for either the Ford or Rockefeller Foundations. Clearly, exhortation has not been successful in increasing foundation professionalism.

The survey of The Conference Board done for the Commission also indicated a similar need for staff in corporate giving. They said that "although professional staff analysis is the most widely used evaluative technique, the fact is that there is a minimum of professional staff employed specifically for the contributions and foundation functions. More than four out of ten companies have no professional or clerical staff. Only one out of four companies has one full time professional working in this area.

"It has been previously noted that a number of corporate leaders (23 per cent) indicated they would increase contributions if they had more confidence that their contributions programs were successful. Perhaps part of the problem lies in this area of professionalization and evaluation. If 41 per cent of the companies lack professional staff, how can they assess the need for new grants, the effectiveness of on-going grants, the performance of donor agencies?"

I therefore recommend that there be a requirement that any organization making grants in excess of $100,000 per year employ at least one full-time professional (i.e., not a bookkeeper, accountant or donor's secretary) or, in the alternative, join in a cooperative venture with other organizations sharing common staff.

Page 170, by GRACIELA OLIVAREZ

The recommendation of the majority of the Commission that tax-exempt organizations should broaden boards and staffs to encourage greater responsiveness to a true community of needs is much too weak an endorsement of a vital national concern. If there exists true interest in accountability and accessibility it will have to be manifested in more than just words in order to be convincing. This is a thorny area which the Commission appears to have bypassed deliberately. Rather than deal with the principles and mechanics involved, it simply relied once again upon exhortation, a practice which for innovation and liberalization of philanthropic giving has failed repeatedly. On the other hand, I recommend that tax-exempt organizations with assets of more than $500,000 and/or gifts of more than $250,000 be required by law to include on their boards of directors members who are representative of the constituency to be served. That is, nonprofit organizations which focus on real issues, for example, should be required to include on their boards an accurate cross-section of the geographic section. Similarly, tax-exempt organizations which support a particular interest, such as music, should include on board membership a spectrum of constituents, and not simply those representing one part of the constituency.

Page 170, by WILLIAM M. ROTH, with which EDWIN D. ETHERINGTON and ELIZABETH J. McCORMACK have asked to be associated

This is an important recommendation, but it should be expanded by adding a more specific reference to the need for far greater participation by women and ethnic minorities and by the recipients of foundation grants on the staffs and boards of foundations. Nonprofit institutions must assume a leadership role in the establishment of effective, affirmative action programs.

Page 170, by MAX M. FISHER, with which LESTER CROWN, RAYMOND J. GALLAGHER, PHILIP M. KLUTZNICK and RALPH LAZARUS have asked to be associated

The recommendation for organizations to broaden their boards must be qualified for special purpose and special constituency organizations. Religious organizations are not expected to become nonsectarian. Special purpose organizations cannot be expected to include people not committed to their purposes. This recommendation applies to broadly based general purpose organizations.

Page 172, by WILLIAM M. ROTH, with which EDWIN D. ETHERINGTON has asked to be associated

The concept of an "independent" foundation is an interesting one, but I believe donor representation should be eliminated entirely before this status is granted.

Page 175, by WILLIAM M. ROTH, with which WALTER A. HAAS, JR. has asked to be associated

Although a 6 per cent payout is larger than the current income of most portfolios and the prospective increase in their capital value may not keep abreast of future inflation, nevertheless I would stay with the present level of payout, although a less ambiguous formula might be devised. The slow dispersal of the corpus of a foundation is not necessarily a bad thing if new ones are being continually created. This, of course, would require a climate in which new growth would take place.

Page 176, by RAYMOND J. GALLAGHER, with which LESTER CROWN has asked to be associated

State governments already adequately police the solicitations of charitable contributions. There is no hard data in the material collected by this Commission that warrants a recommendation that the federal government assume a new policy role in this area. The Commission indicates that it believes that the vast majority of charitable solicitations are conscientiously and economically undertaken. The Commission, however, is con-

220

cerned about the impression of many taxpayers that charity solicitations cost more than they should. I do not believe that the effective remedy for this impression is the creation of a new federal bureaucracy or the expansion of an existing one. Potential donors who have doubts about the efficiency of charitable solicitations can inquire directly of the organizations they are concerned about; and if they are not satisfied with the answers they are given, they have the most effective remedy of all: not making the contribution.

Page 179, by MAX M. FISHER, with which LESTER CROWN, RAYMOND J. GALLAGHER, PHILIP M. KLUTZNICK and RALPH LAZARUS have asked to be associated

This is overstated. Only the smallest fraction of philanthropic agencies have any lobbyists in Washington at any time.

Page 191, by GEORGE ROMNEY, with which LESTER CROWN, RAYMOND J. GALLAGHER, PHILIP M. KLUTZNICK and JOHN M. MUSSER have asked to be associated

The priority need for strengthening the nonprofit sector is not an expansion of the role of government, as proposed in this report, but a strengthening of the nonprofit sector's capacity to initiate and implement joint action. This Commission is itself evidence of that need.

The intense competition among the separate nonprofit organizations for funds, volunteers, recognition and survival has thus far prevented the degree of cooperation required to enable them to do jointly what they cannot do as well, or at all, separately. Many of the functions proposed in this report to be performed by a "permanent national commission for the nonprofit sector" could be better executed by a recognized and supported private instrument. Indeed the creation of this "national commisson" by Congress is likely to lead to governmental intervention in the private nonprofit sector that will weaken it rather than strengthen it. The likelihood of this outcome is increased as long as the nonprofit sector lacks any organized means of asserting and protecting its common interests.

221

Page 191, by RAYMOND J. GALLAGHER, with which LESTER CROWN has asked to be associated

I respectfully dissent from the recommendation of the Commission that a permanent national commission on the nonprofit sector be established by Congress. Neither our national experience in the nonprofit area nor the data collected by this Commission warrants the establishment of a permanent national commission on the nonprofit sector by an Act of Congress with authority in the commission to require annual financial reports by exempt organizations and to propose various types of standards of nonprofit behavior. All such a national commission would do is increase the administratrive costs of nonprofit organizations, thus reducing funds available for their beneficiaries. Far from aiding these institutions, the national commission will be another financial drain and another administrative burden. In addition, the commission would provide direct federal regulation and supervision of churches and other religious organizations. There is no way to avoid the fact that this recommendation would create a "watchdog" bureaucracy armed with the force of legal compulsion to supervise the practice of religious freedom in the United States.

Page 192, by MAX M. FISHER, with which RALPH LAZARUS has asked to be associated

No reference is made in the recommendation on the selection of the members of the proposed permanent commission to the essential element of the Commission sub-committee's report providing for an advisory body representing a cross-section of the philanthropic fields themselves, and that the twelve members were to be drawn from those fields on the recommendation of the advisory body. The membership of the commission is crucial. As the report now stands, it does not include the critically essential requirement regarding the membership of the commission, with that expertness of philanthropic experience. It was this provision which persuaded at least some members of the Commission to support the recommendation for a permanent commission.

APPENDIX I

COMMISSION STUDIES

The following are the titles and authors of all studies, reports and analyses undertaken for or by the Commission, arranged according to subject matter. The works themselves are published separately in the Compendium of Commission research.

I. COMMISSION RECOMMENDATIONS

Analysis of the Recommendations of the Commission on Private Philanthropy and Public Needs, Including Means of Implementation

Commission Staff

II. HISTORY, TRENDS AND CURRENT MAGNITUDES

Private Philanthropy and Public Needs: An Historical Perspective
Prof. Robert H. Bremner, Department of History, Ohio State University

Private Giving in the American Economy: 1960-1972
Prof. Ralph L. Nelson, Department of Economics, Queens College of the City of New York

Scope of the Private Voluntary Charitable Sector, 1974
Gabriel G. Rudney, Assistant Director, Office of Tax Analysis, U.S. Department of the Treasury

Results from Two National Surveys of Philanthropic Activity
Prof. James N. Morgan, Richard F. Dye, Judith H. Hybels, Institute for Social Research, University of Michigan

Employment and Earnings in the Nonprofit Charitable Sector
Prof. T. Nicolaus Tideman, Department of Economics, Virginia Polytechnic Institute and State University, Blacksburg, Va.

The Size of the Voluntary Nonprofit Sector: Concepts and Measures
Prof. Burton A. Weisbrod, Department of Economics, University of Wisconsin, Stephen H. Long, Department of Economics, Franklin Marshall College, Lancaster, Pa.

A Study of Religious Receipts and Expenditures in the United States
Interfaith Research Committee of the Commission on Private Philanthropy and Public Needs, Stuart M. Lewis, Project Coordinator

III. PHILANTHROPIC FIELDS OF INTEREST

A. Education

Private Philanthropy and Higher Education: History, Current Impact and Public
Policy Considerations
  Prof. Earl F. Cheit, School of Business Administration, University of California,
  Berkeley, Theodore E. Lobman III, Post Doctoral Fellow, Carnegie Council on
  Policy Studies in Higher Education, Berkeley, Calif.

Philanthropy in Higher Education: A Study of the Impact of Voluntary Support on
College and University Income
  Dr. Hans H. Jenny, Vice President for Finance and Business, College of Wooster,
  Wooster, Ohio, Mary Ann Allan, Research Assistant, Dundee, New York

Philanthropy, Public Needs and Nonpublic Schools
  Prof. Donald A. Erickson, Faculty of Education, Simon Fraser University, Burnaby, B.C., Canada

The Nonpublic School and Private Philanthropy
  Dr. Robert L. Lamborn, Executive Director, Council for American Private Education, Washington, D.C.; Cary Potter, President, National Association of Independent Schools, Boston; Dr. Al H. Senske, Secretary of Elementary and Secondary
  Schools, Board of Parish Education, Lutheran Church-Missouri Synod, St. Louis

B. Science

The Role of Private Philanthropy and Public Support of Science in the United
States
  Dr. Caryl P. Haskins, Former President, Carnegie Institution of Washington, D.C.

C. Health

The Changing Role of Private Philanthropy in Health Affairs
  Dr. Robert J. Blendon, Vice President, The Robert Wood Johnson Foundation,
  Princeton, N.J.

D. Welfare

Some Aspects of Evolving Social Policy in Relation to Private Philanthropy
  Wilbur J. Cohen, Dean, School of Education, University of Michigan

Some Aspects of Private Philanthropy in Relation to Social Welfare
  Dr. Ellen Winston, Author on social welfare issues, Raleigh, N.C.

The Voluntary Social Agency Experiments, Innovates, Demonstrates and Influences
Public Social Policy: The Community Service Society of New York 1930-1970
  Dr. Joseph L. Vigilante, Dean, and Dr. Ruth Kantrow, School of Social Work,
  Adelphi University, Garden City, N.Y.

Social Welfare
  Alvin L. Schorr, General Director, Community Service Society of New York, Dr.
  Rose Dobrof, School of Social Work, Hunter College, New York

E. Arts and Culture

A Report on the Arts
  Caroline Hightower, Editor and writer, New York

F. Environment

The Role of Private Philanthropy in Relation to Environment—Pollution
  Blair T. Bower, Consultant, Resources for the Future, Washington, D.C.

The Role of Philanthropy in the Environmental Field: Preservation of Natural Lands and Historic Properties
  Janet Koch, Writer, New York, Thomas W. Richards, President, Hartzog, Lader and Richards, Environmental Consultants

G. Voluntarism and Community Action

A Report on Voluntary Activities and Leadership Opinion
  National Center for Voluntary Action: Thomas D. Queisser, Deputy Executive Director; George E. Chalmers, Report Project Director

A Study of the Quantity of Volunteer Activity of United Way and its Member Agencies
  United Way of America

A Philanthropic Profile of Five Cities: Atlanta, Cleveland, Des Moines, Hartford, San Francisco
  Victor Weingarten, President, Institute of Public Affairs, Inc.

The Anatomy of Giving: Five American Cities
  Bice Clemow, Editor, West Hartford, Conn.
  "Private Philanthropy in Des Moines"
    —Calvin Kentfield
  "Passing the Buck: Philanthropy in San Francisco"
    —Jack Shepherd
  "Cleveland: Faint Halo Around a Solid Tradition of Giving"
    —Robert S. Merriman
  "Money Above, Action Below: Philanthropy in Hartford"
    —Vivian Gornick
  "Search for the Bridge: The Stand-off Between City Hall and 'Five Points' in Atlanta"
    —Bice Clemow

H. Social Action

An Agenda For the Future
  Reynold Levy and Waldemar A. Nielsen,
  Aspen Institute for Humanistic Studies

Philanthrophy and the Powerless
  Sarah C. Carey, Cladouhas and Brashares,
  Washington, D.C.

Who's Funding the Women's Movement?
  Mary Jean Tully, President, NOW Legal Defense and Education Fund

The New Federalism, Government Accountability and Philanthropy
  Peter J. Petkas, Director, Southern Governmental Monitoring Project, Southern Regional Council, Inc.

Patterns of Class and Ethnic Discrimination by Private Philanthropy
  Msgr. Geno Baroni, Founder and President, Arthur Naparstek, Director of Public Policy and Program Development, Karen Kollias, Policy Analyst, The National Center for Urban Ethnic Affairs

Values, Voluntary Action and Philanthropy: The Appropriate Relationship of Private Philanthropy to Public Needs
  David Horton Smith, Associate Professor, Department of Sociology, Boston College

The Role of Foundations in Broadcasting and Cable Communications Policy Development
   Albert H. Kramer, National Citizens Committee for Broadcasting, Washington, D.C.

The Role of the United Way in Philanthropy
   David Horton Smith, Associate Professor, Department of Sociology, Boston College

Foundation Grants to Corporate Activist Groups: The Donee Perspective
   Phillip W. Moore, Easton, Md.

Public Needs, Public Policy and Philanthropy
   Thomas R. Asher, Executive Director, Study of Political Influence, Washington, D.C.

I. Public Affairs and International Activities

Philanthropic Activity in International Affairs
   Prof. Adam Yarmolinsky, Ralph Waldo Emerson
   University Professor, University of Massachusetts

The Role of Private Philanthropy in Public Affairs
   Paul N. Ylvisaker, Dean, Graduate School of Education, Harvard University, and
   Jane H. Mavity, New York

IV. SPECIAL BEHAVIORAL STUDIES

A. Income Tax

Tax Incentives and Charitable Contributions in the United States: A Microeconometric Analysis
   Prof. Martin S. Feldstein, Department of Economics, Harvard University

Estimating Separate Price Elasticities by Income Class
   Prof. Martin S. Feldstein, Department of Economics, Harvard University

The Income Tax and Charitable Contributions: Estimates and Simulations with the Treasury Tax Files
   Prof. Martin S. Feldstein and Dr. Amy Taylor, Department of Economics, Harvard University

Effects of the Charitable Deduction on Contributions by Low Income and Middle Income Households: Evidence from the National Survey of Philanthropy
   Prof. Michael J. Boskin, Department of Economics, Stanford University, and Prof. Martin S. Feldstein, Department of Economics, Harvard University

B. Estate Tax

Estate Taxation and Charitable Bequests
   Prof. Michael J. Boskin, Department of Economics, Stanford University, and National Bureau of Economic Research

Charitable Bequests, Estate Taxation and Intergenerational Wealth Transfers
   Prof. Martin S. Feldstein, Department of Economics, Harvard University

C. Non-Economic Motivations

Non-Economic Motivational Factors in Philanthropic Behavior
   Dr. Fred R. Crawford, Director, Center for Research in Social Change, Emory University, Atlanta

V. GOVERNMENT FUNDING OF VOLUNTARY ORGANI-ZATIONS

VI. TAXES AND REGULATION

227

Legal Aspects of Charitable Contributions of Appreciated Property to Public Charities
   Harry K. Mansfield, Ronald L. Groves, Ropes & Gray, Boston

Treatment of Volunteer Services and Related Expenses Under the Internal Revenue Code
   Edmund C. Bennett, Tillinghast, Collins & Graham, Providence, R.I.

D. Estate Tax Incentives

Estate Tax Deduction for Charitable Benefits: Proposed Limitations
   John Holt Myers, Williams, Myers and Quiggle, Washington, D.C.

Dimensions of Charitable Giving Reported on Federal Estate, Gift and Fiduciary Tax Returns
   Emil M. Sunley, Jr., The Brookings Institution, Washington, D.C.

Death, Taxes and Charitable Bequests: A Survey of Issues and Options
   Prof. Richard E. Wagner, Department of Economics, Virginia Polytechnic Institute and State University, Blacksburg, Va.

Proposed Limitations on the Estate Tax Deduction for Charitable Transfers
   Prof. David Westfall, Harvard University Law School

E. Property Tax Incentives

The Exemption of Religious, Educational and Charitable Institutions from Property Taxation
   Dr. John F. Shannon, Assistant Director, Dr. L. Richard Gabler, Senior Analyst, Advisory Commission on Intergovernmental Relations

F. Non-Tax Incentives

Alternative Approaches to Encouraging Philanthropic Activities
   Prof. Gerard M. Brannon, Department of Economics, Georgetown University, and James Strnad, Tax Analysts and Advocates, Washington, D.C.

A Tax by Any Other Name: The Donor Directed Automatic Percentage Contribution Bonus, A Budget Alternative for Financing Governmental Support of Charity
   Aaron Wildavsky, Dean, Graduate School of Public Policy, and Prof. David Good, Department of Economics, University of California, Berkeley

Study of Federal Matching Grants for Charitable Contributions
   Prof. Paul R. McDaniel, Law School, Boston College

G. Oversight and Regulation

Federal Oversight of Private Philanthropy
   David Ginsburg, Lee R. Marks, Ronald P. Wertheim, Ginsburg, Feldman and Bress, Washington, D.C.

Criteria for Exemption Under Section 501(c)(3)
   John P. Persons, John J. Osborn, Jr., Charles F. Feldman, Patterson, Belknap & Webb, New York

An Analysis of the Federal Tax Distinctions Between Public and Private Charitable Organizations
   Laurens Williams, Sutherland, Asbill & Brennan, Washington, D.C., and Donald V. Moorehead, Chief Minority Counsel, Committee on Finance, U.S. Senate (formerly Sutherland, Asbill & Brennan)

Legislative Activities of Charitable Organizations Other Than Private Foundations with Addendum on Legislative Activities of Private Foundations
   John B. Huffaker, Pepper, Hamilton & Scheetz, Philadelphia

229

APPENDIX II

MEMBERS OF THE COMMISSION

The following identifications of Commission members include, where appropriate, both a principal occupation and a major voluntary sector affiliation.

Chairman
John H. Filer
Chairman, Aetna Life & Casualty
Hartford, Conn.
    Director, Hartford Institute of Criminal and Social Justice

Executive Director
Leonard L. Silverstein
Silverstein and Mullens
Washington, D.C.
    Director, National Symphony Orchestra Association

William H. Bowen
President, Commercial National Bank
Little Rock, Ark.
    Director, Arkansas Association of Private Colleges

Lester Crown
President, Material Service Corporation
Chicago
    Trustee, Northwestern University

C. Douglas Dillon
Chairman, U. S. & Foreign Securities Corp.
New York
    President, Metropolitan Museum of Art

232

233

William Matson Roth
Regent, University of California
San Francisco
   Chairman, San Francisco Museum of Art

Althea T. L. Simmons
Director for Education Programs
NAACP Special Contribution Fund
New York

The Rev. Leon H. Sullivan
Pastor, Zion Baptist Church
Philadelphia

David B. Truman
President, Mount Holyoke College
South Hadley, Mass.

APPENDIX III

COMMISSION CONSULTANTS AND ADVISORS

Consultants

Howard A. Bolton
Milbank, Tweed, Hadley & McCloy
New York

Wade Greene
Writer and Editor
Editor and principal writer of the Commission's report

Waldemar A. Nielsen
Director of Program on Problems of American Pluralism
Aspen Institute for Humanistic Studies

Stanley S. Surrey
Jeremiah Smith Professor of Law
Harvard University Law School

Adam Yarmolinsky
Ralph Waldo Emerson University Professor
University of Massachusetts

Paul N. Ylvisaker
Dean, Graduate School of Education
Harvard University

Special Consultants

James W. Abernathy
Director of Research
Grantsmanship Center

Martin S. Feldstein
Professor of Economics
Harvard University

Theodore J. Jacobs
Former Director, Center for Study of Responsive Law

Porter McKeever
Associate, John D. Rockefeller 3rd

Ralph L. Nelson
Professor of Economics
Queens College, City University of New York

John J. Schwartz
President
American Association of Fund-Raising Counsel

Sally J. Shroyer
New York

Carlton E. Spitzer
Vice President
T. J. Ross & Associates
Washington, D. C.

ADVISORY COMMITTEE

Kenneth L. Albrecht
Assistant Vice President,
  Corporate Affairs
Equitable Life Assurance Society
  of the U.S.
New York

William D. Andrews
Harvard University Law School

Thomas R. Asher
Executive Director
Study of Political Influence
Washington, D.C.

R. Palmer Baker, Jr.
Lord, Day & Lord
New York

Msgr. Geno Baroni
The National Center for
  Urban Ethnic Affairs
Washington, D.C.

Kirk R. Batzer
Coopers & Lybrand
New York

Edmund C. Bennett
Tillinghast, Collins & Graham
Providence, R.I.

Philip Bernstein
Executive Vice President
Council of Jewish Federations
  and Welfare Funds, Inc.
New York

236

Richard M. Bird
Institute of Policy Analysis
University of Toronto

Boris I. Bittker
Yale University Law School

Robert J. Blendon
Vice President for Planning
  and Development
Robert Wood Johnson Foundation
Princeton, N.J.

Walter J. Blum
University of Chicago Law School
Chicago

Henry M. Boetinger
Director of Corporate Planning
American Telephone & Telegraph
New York

Michael J. Boskin
Department of Economics
Stanford University

Blair T. Bower
North Arlington, Virginia

Gerard M. Brannon
Department of Economics
Georgetown University

George F. Break
Department of Economics
University of California, Berkeley

Robert H. Bremner
Department of History
Ohio State University

Henry R. Brett
Corporate Contributions Counselor
Standard Oil Company of California
San Francisco

Sarah C. Carey
Cladouhas and Brashares
Washington, D.C.

Earl F. Cheit
Associate Director
Carnegie Council on Policy Studies
  in Higher Education
Berkeley, Calif.

Carl C. Clark
Commission for the Advancement of
  Public Interest Organizations
Washington, D.C.

Bice Clemow
Editor
West Hartford, Conn.

Edwin S. Cohen
University of Virginia Law School

Sheldon S. Cohen
Cohen and Uretz
Washington, D.C.

Wilbur J. Cohen
Dean
School of Education
University of Michigan
Ann Arbor

Marvin K. Collie
Vinson, Elkins, Searls, Connally
  & Smith
Houston, Texas

Fred R. Crawford
Department of Humanities
Emory University
Atlanta

Charles W. Davis
Hopkins, Sutter, Owen, Mulroy
  & Davis
Chicago

Delford W. Edens
Haskins & Sells
New York

Donald A. Erickson
Department of Education
Simon-Fraser University
Burnaby, B.C.

Marion R. Fremont-Smith
Choate, Hall & Stewart
Boston

F. Daniel Frost
Gibson, Dunn & Crutcher
Los Angeles

David Ginsburg
Ginsburg, Feldman and Bress
Washington, D.C.

Robert F. Goheen
Chairman, Council on Foundations, Inc.
New York

S. Peter Goldberg
Council of Jewish Federations
  and Welfare Funds, Inc.
New York

Arthur Jack Grimes
American Institute of Biological
  Sciences
Arlington, Va.

237

238

Rev. Robert V. Monticello
Associate General Secretary
United States Catholic Conference
Washington, D.C.

Phillip W. Moore
Easton, Md.

James N. Morgan
Survey Research Center
University of Michigan

Robert H. Mulreany
DeForest & Duer
New York

John Holt Myers
Williams, Myers and Quiggle
Washington, D.C.

Michael K. Newton
President
Associated Council of the Arts
New York

John S. Nolan
Miller & Chevalier
Washington, D.C.

Joseph M. Paul
Assistant Chief
Charitable Foundations Section
Office of the Attorney General
State of Ohio
Columbus

Joseph A. Pechman
The Brookings Institution
Washington, D.C.

John P. Persons
Patterson, Belknap & Webb
New York

Peter J. Petkas
Director
Southern Governmental
  Monitoring Project
Southern Regional Council
Atlanta

Timothy J. Racek
Arthur Andersen & Co.
New York

Thomas W. Richards
National Trust for Historic Preservation
Washington, D.C.

Harold Roser
Manager, Community Development
  Programs
Exxon Corporation
New York

Alvin L. Schorr
Community Service Society,
  of New York
New York

John F. Shannon
Assistant Director
Advisory Commission on
  Intergovernmental Relations
Washington, D.C.

Ira Silverman
Executive Director
Institute for Jewish Policy Planning
  and Research
Washington, D.C.

John G. Simon
Yale University Law School

David Horton Smith
Department of Sociology
Boston College

Donald R. Spuehler
O'Melveny & Myers
Los Angeles

J. John Stevenson
Chief
Charitable Foundations Section
Office of the Attorney General
State of Ohio
Columbus

Lawrence M. Stone
School of Law
University of California, Berkeley

Norman A. Sugarman
Baker, Hostetler & Patterson
Cleveland

Emil M. Sunley, Jr.
The Brookings Institution
Washington, D.C.

Wayne E. Thompson
Senior Vice President
Dayton-Hudson Corporation
Minneapolis

T. Nicolaus Tideman
Department of Economics
Virginia Polytechnic Institute
  and State University
Blacksburg, Va.

Thomas A. Troyer
Caplin & Drysdale
Washington, D.C.

Mary Jean Tully
President
NOW Legal Defense and Education
  Fund
New York

John H. Vandenberg
Assistant to Council of the Twelve
Salt Lake City

Thomas Vasquez
Financial Economist
U.S. Department of the Treasury
Washington, D.C.

Joseph L. Vigilante
Dean
School of Social Work
Adelphi University
Garden City, N.Y.

Richard E. Wagner
Center for Study of Public Choice
Virginia Polytechnic Institute
  and State University
Blacksburg, Va.

John A. Wallace
King & Spalding
Atlanta

Victor Weingarten
President
Institute of Public Affairs, Inc.
New York

Burton A. Weisbrod
Department of Economics
University of Wisconsin
Madison, Wisc.

David Westfall
Harvard University Law School

A.M. Wiggins, Jr.
Reed Smith Shaw & McClay
Pittsburgh

Aaron Wildavsky
Dean, Graduate School of Public Policy
University of California, Berkeley

Laurens Williams (Deceased)
Sutherland, Asbill & Brennan
Washington, D.C.

Ellen Winston
Raleigh, N.C.

Bernard Wolfman
Center for Advanced Study in the
  Behavioral Sciences
Stanford, Calif.

Raul Yzaguirre
Executive Director
National Council of La Raza
Washington, D.C.